INSTANT Piano Songs

Audio Access Included

HITS OF 2010-2019
Simple Sheet Music + Audio Play-Along

PLAYBACK+
Speed • Pitch • Balance • Loop

To access audio visit:
www.halleonard.com/mylibrary

Enter Code
4065-1514-8126-3248

ISBN 978-1-5400-9182-6

Visit Hal Leonard Online at
www.halleonard.com

T0026091

Contact us:
Hal Leonard
7777 West Bluemound Road
Milwaukee, WI 53213
Email: info@halleonard.com

In Europe, contact:
Hal Leonard Europe Limited
42 Wigmore Street
Marylebone, London, W1U 2RN
Email: info@halleonardeurope.com

In Australia, contact:
Hal Leonard Australia Pty. Ltd.
4 Lentara Court
Cheltenham, Victoria, 3192 Australia
Email: info@halleonard.com.au

CONTENTS

Welcome to the *INSTANT Piano Songs* series!

This unique, flexible collection allows you to play with either one hand or two. Three playing options are available—all of which sound great with the online backing tracks:

1. **Play only the melody with your right hand.**

2. **Add basic chords in your left hand, which are notated for you.**

3. **Use suggested rhythm patterns for the left-hand chords.**

Letter names appear inside the notes in both hands to assist you, and there are no key signatures to worry about. If a **sharp** ♯ or **flat** ♭ is needed, it is shown beside the note each time, even within the same measure.

If two notes are connected by a **tie** ‿, hold the first note for the combined number of beats. (The second note does not show a letter name since it is not re-struck.)

Sometimes the melody needs to be played an octave higher to avoid overlapping with the left-hand chords. (If your starting note is C, the next C to the right is one octave higher.) If you are using only your right hand, however, you can disregard this instruction in the music.

🔊 The backing tracks are designed to enhance the piano arrangements, regardless of how you choose to play them. Each track includes two measures of count-off clicks at the beginning. If the recording is too fast or too slow, use the online **PLAYBACK+** player to adjust it to a more comfortable tempo (speed).

Optional left-hand rhythm patterns are provided for when you are ready to move beyond the basic chords. The patterns are based on the three notes of the basic chords and appear as small, gray notes in the first line of each song. Feel free to use the suggested pattern throughout the song, or create your own. Sample rhythm patterns are shown below. (Of course, you can always play just the basic chords if you wish!)

Have fun! Whether you play with one hand or two, you'll sound great!

Sample Rhythm Patterns

4/4 Meter

3/4 Meter

6/8 Meter

Also Available

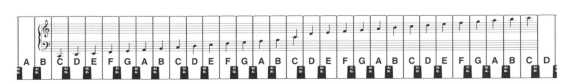

Hal Leonard Student Keyboard Guide HL00296039

Key Stickers HL00100016

All About That Bass

Words and Music by Kevin Kadish
and Meghan Trainor

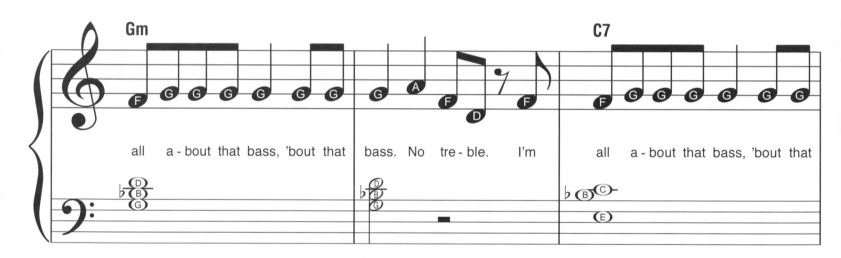

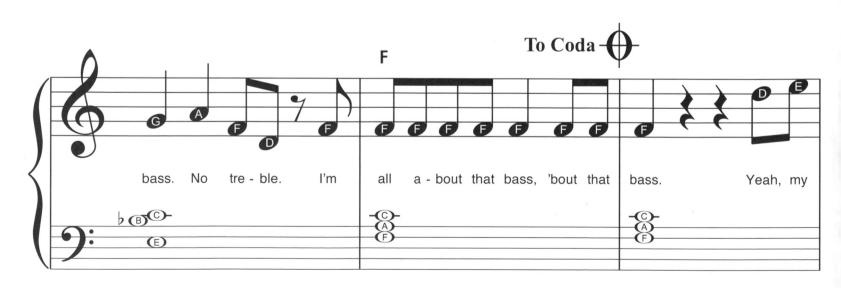

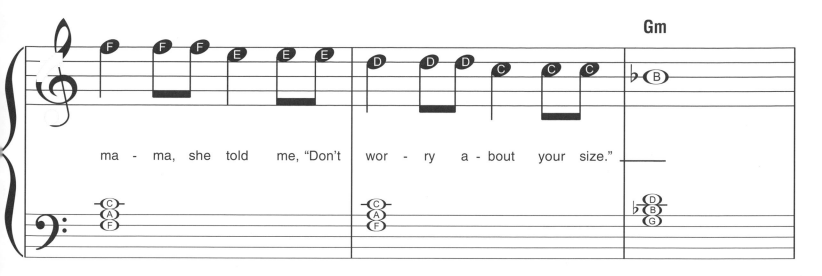

ma - ma, she told me, "Don't wor - ry a - bout your size." ___

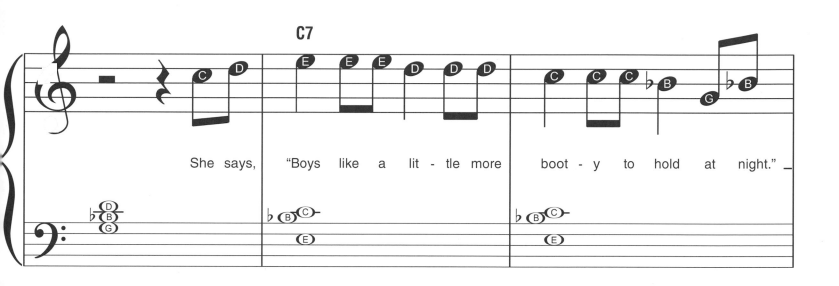

She says, "Boys like a lit - tle more boot - y to hold at night." ___

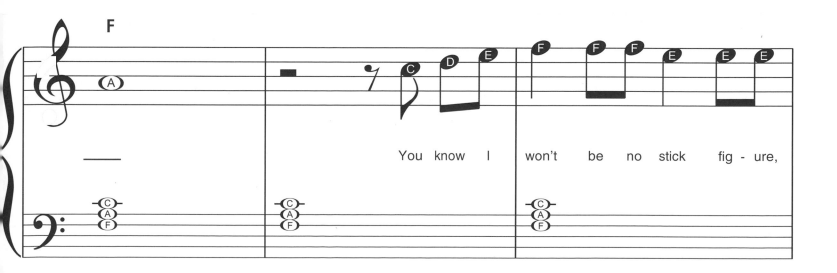

___ You know I won't be no stick fig - ure,

8

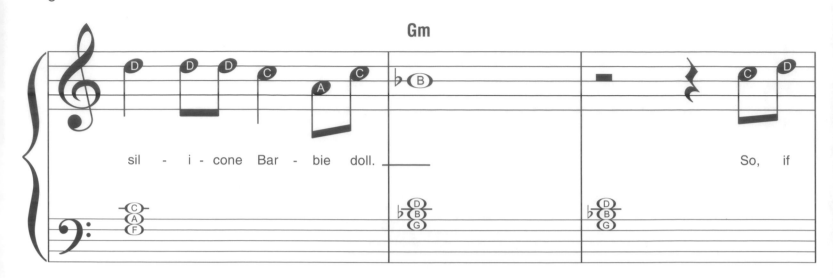

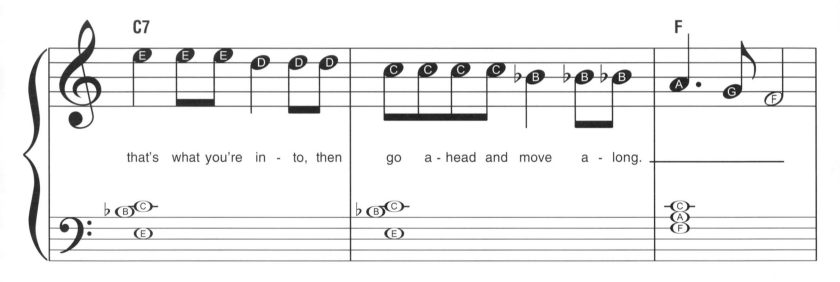

D.S. al Coda
(Return to 𝄋, play to ⊕ and skip to Coda)

CODA

All of Me

Words and Music by John Stephens
and Toby Gad

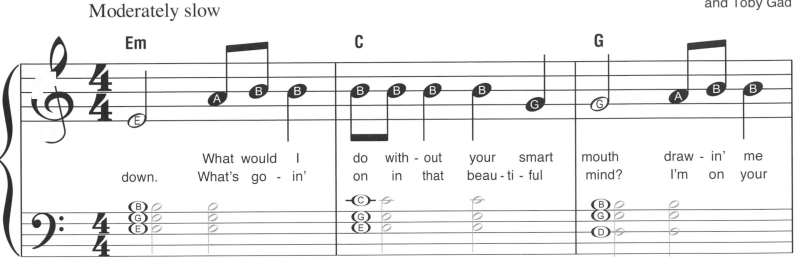

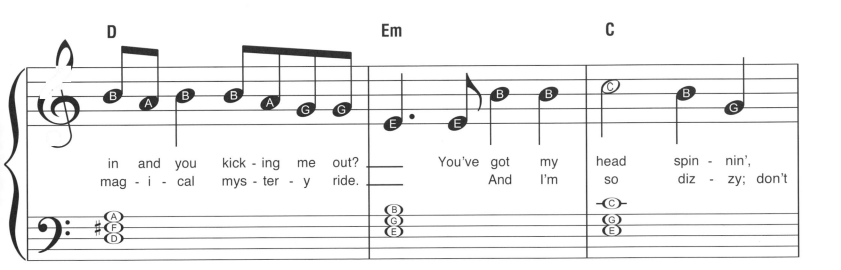

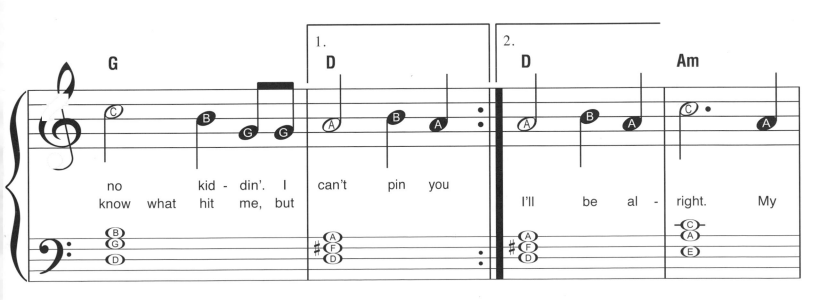

10

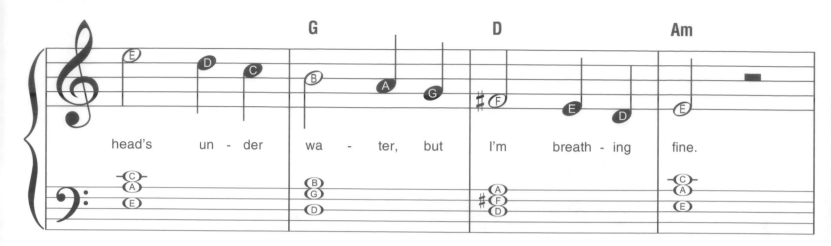

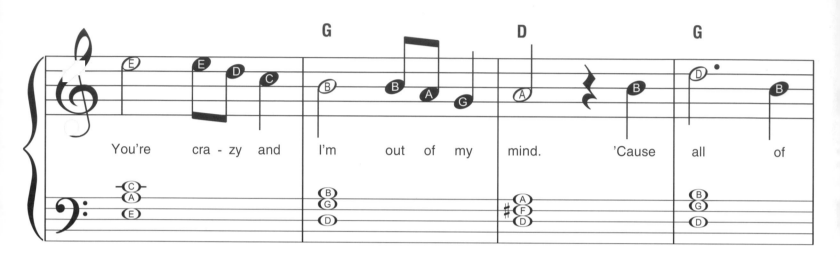

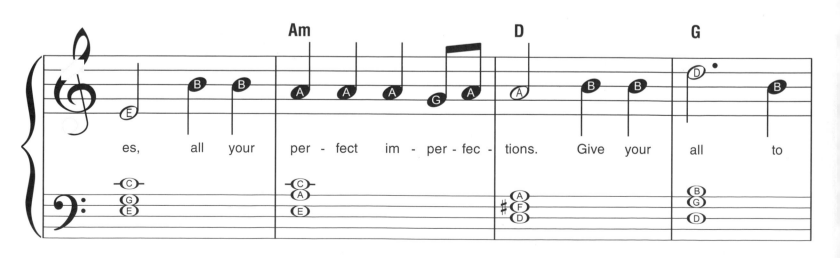

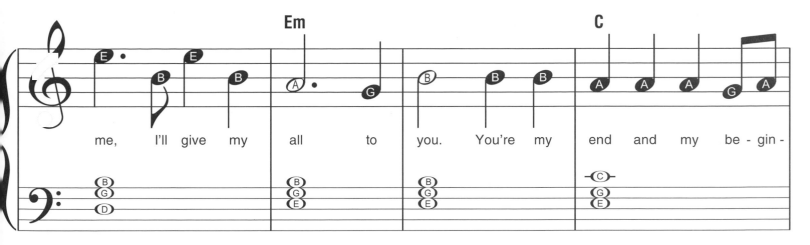

me, I'll give my all to you. You're my end and my be - gin -

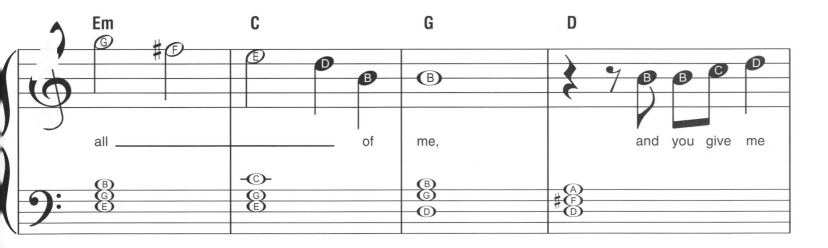

ing. E - ven when I lose, I'm win - ning. 'Cause I give you

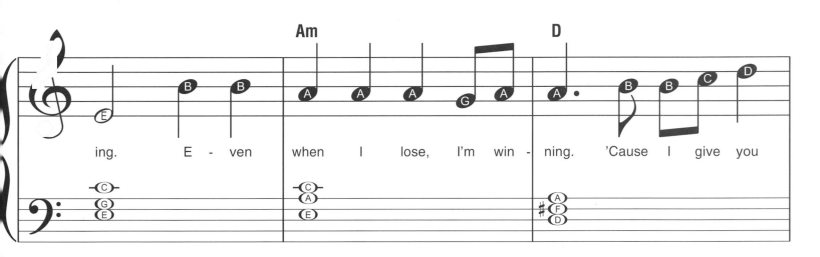

all _____ of me, and you give me

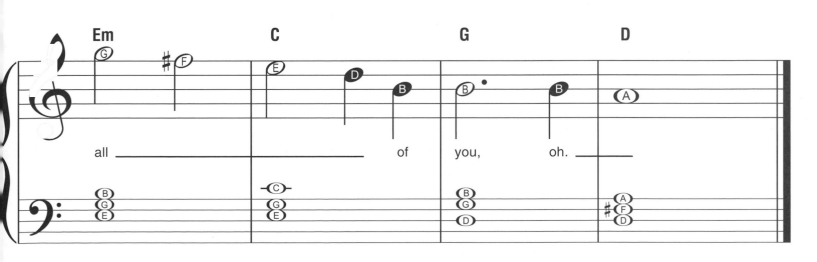

all _____ of you, oh. _____

Budapest

Words and Music by George Barnett
and Joel Pott

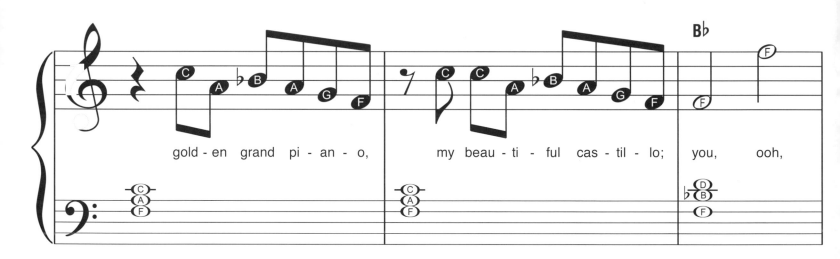

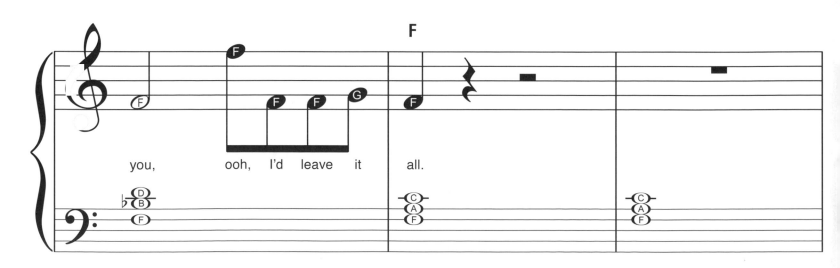

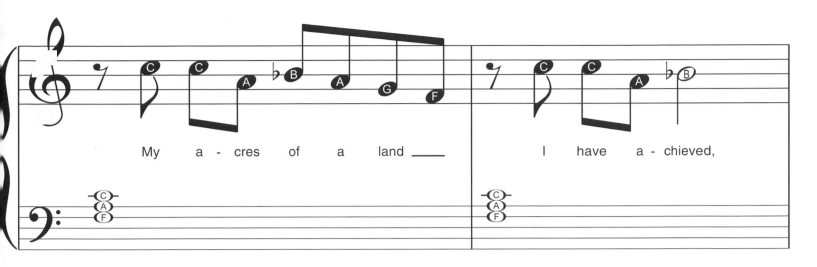

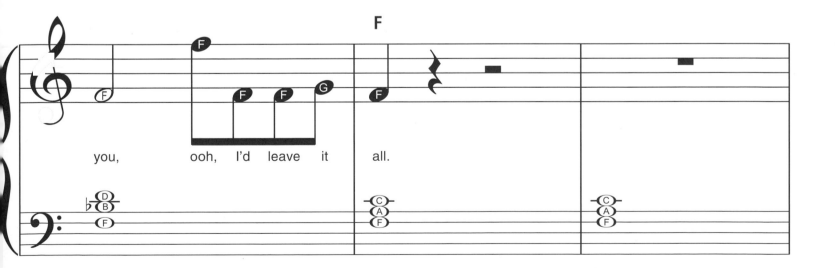

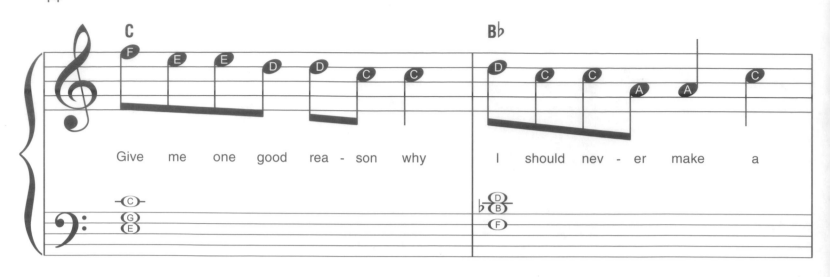

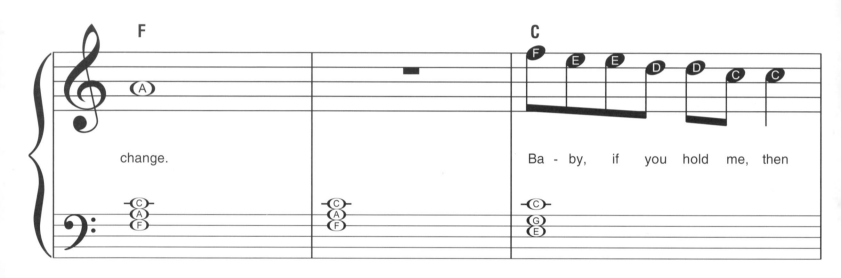

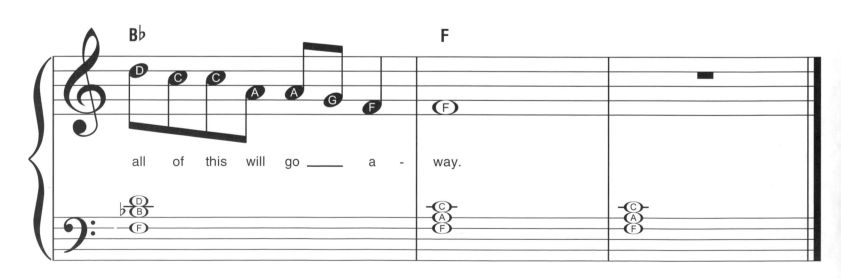

Can't Stop the Feeling!
from TROLLS

Words and Music by Justin Timberlake,
Max Martin and Shellback

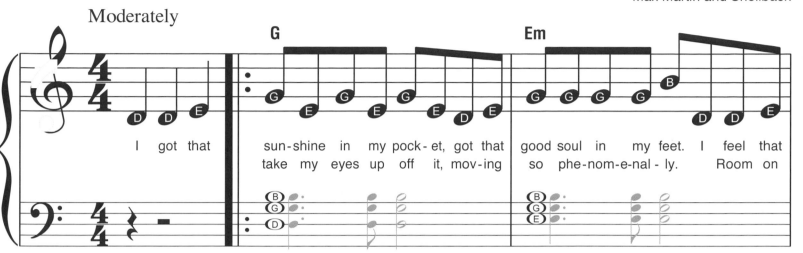

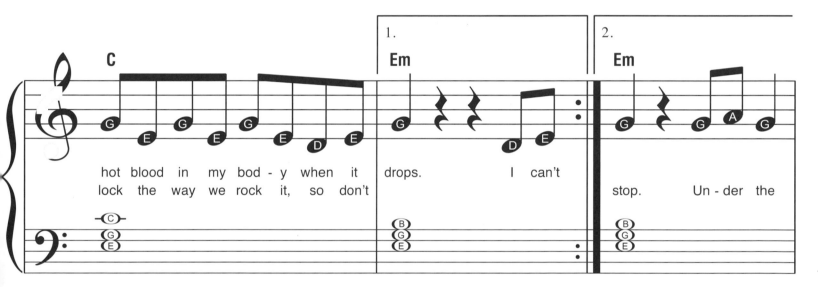

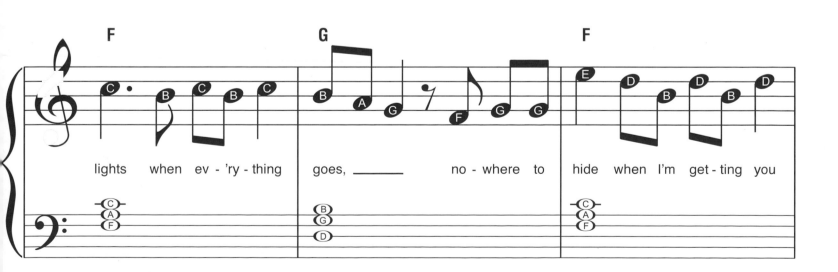

16

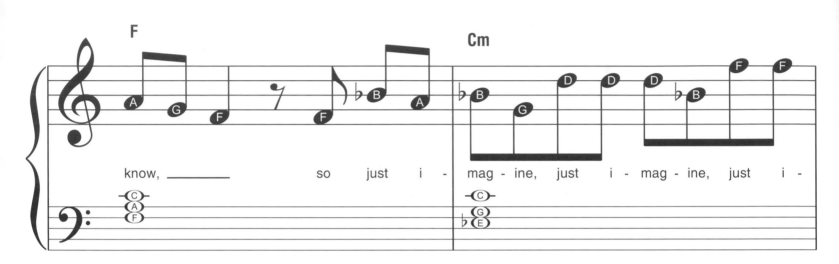

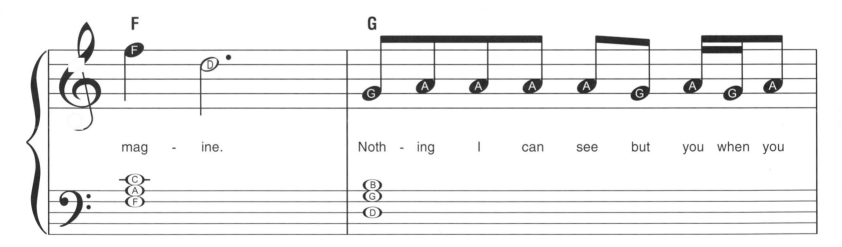

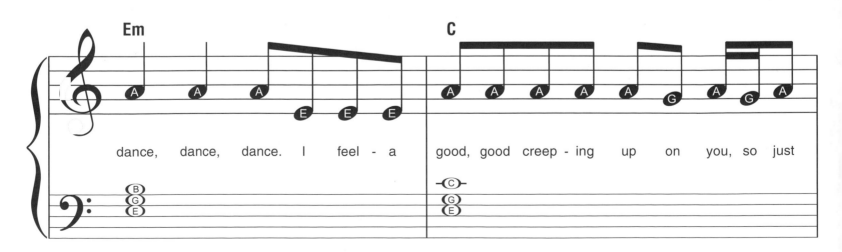

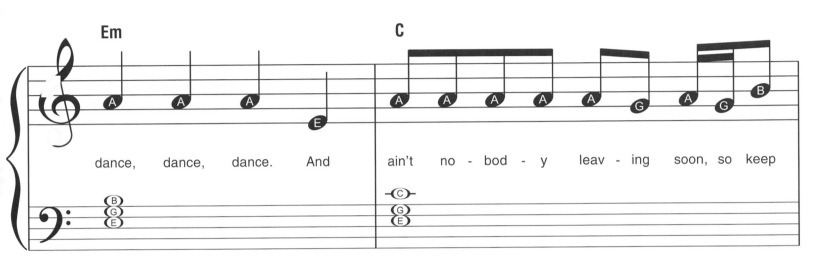

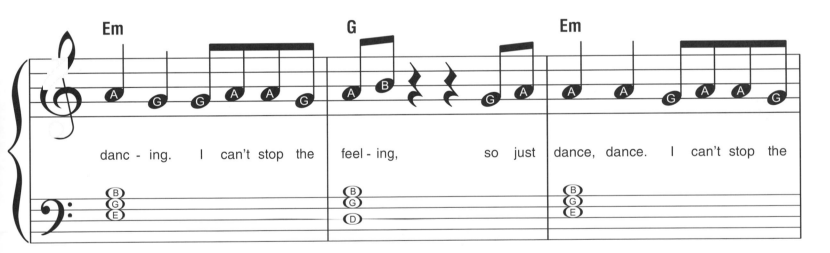

City of Stars
from LA LA LAND

Music by Justin Hurwitz
Lyrics by Benj Pasek & Justin Paul

Moderate Shuffle

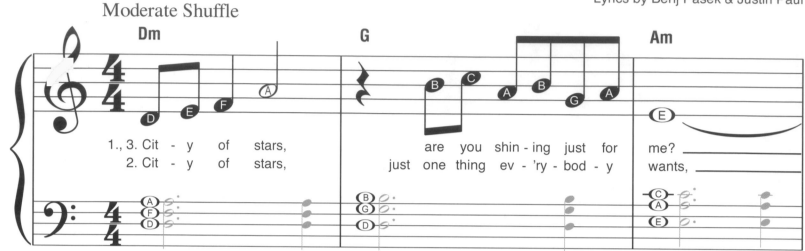

1., 3. Cit - y of stars, are you shin - ing just for me? _____
2. Cit - y of stars, just one thing ev - 'ry - bod - y wants, _____

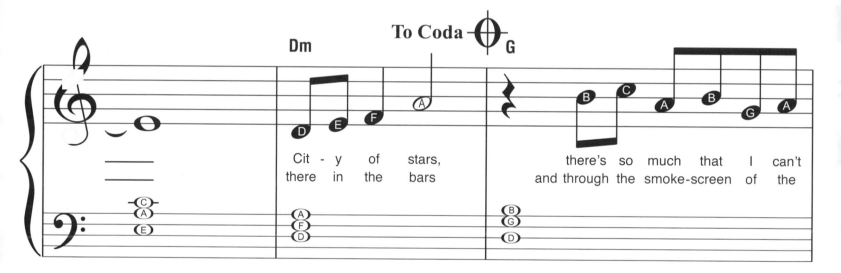

_____ City of stars, there's so much that I can't
_____ there in the bars and through the smoke-screen of the

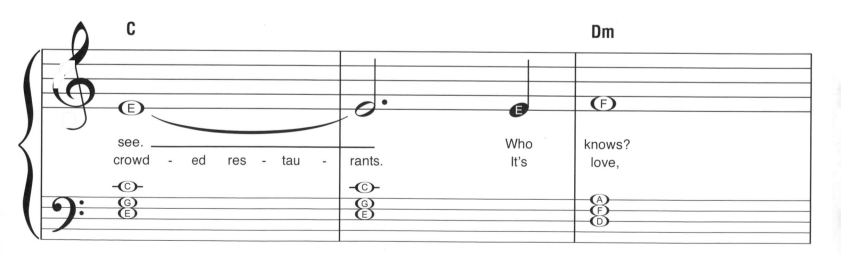

see. _____ Who knows?
crowd - ed res - tau - rants. It's knows? love,

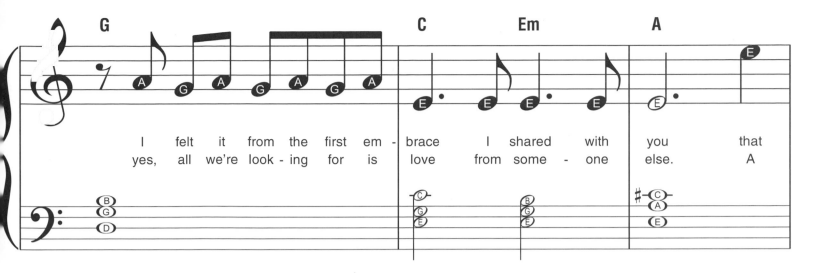

I felt it from the first em - brace I shared with you. that
yes, all we're look - ing for is love from some - one else. A

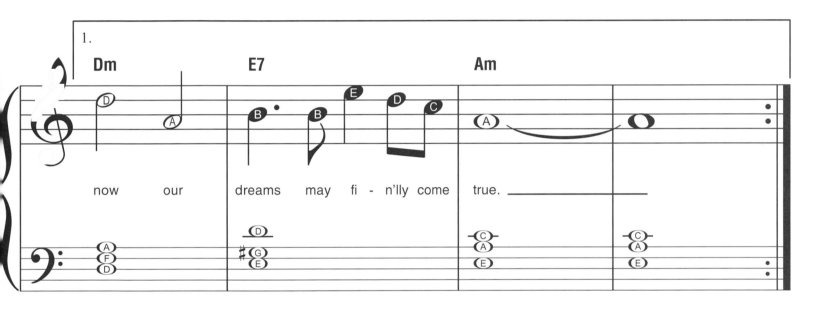

1.
now our dreams may fi - n'lly come true. _____

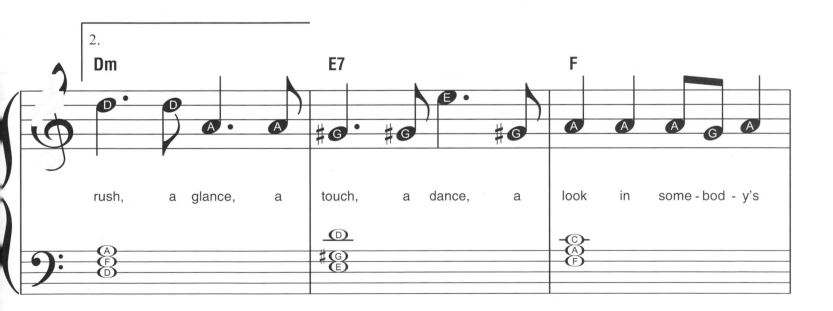

2.
rush, a glance, a touch, a dance, a look in some - bod - y's

20

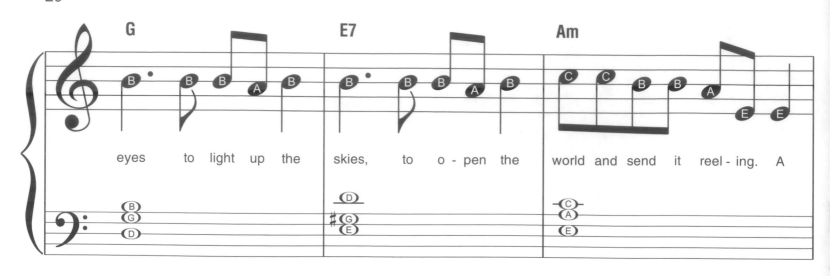

eyes   to light up the   skies,   to o - pen the   world and send it reel - ing. A

D.C. al Coda
(Return to beginning,
play to ⊕ and skip to Coda)

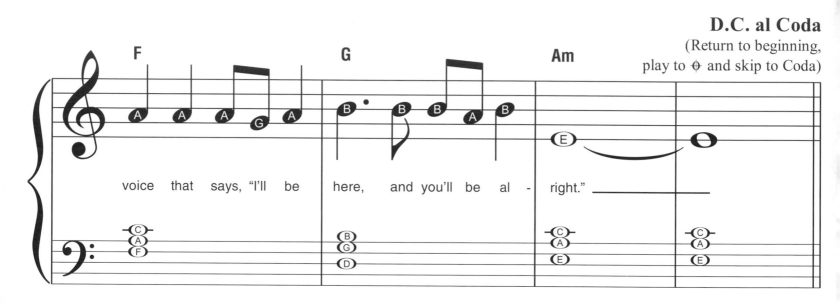

voice that says, "I'll be   here,   and you'll be al - right." _____

CODA ⊕

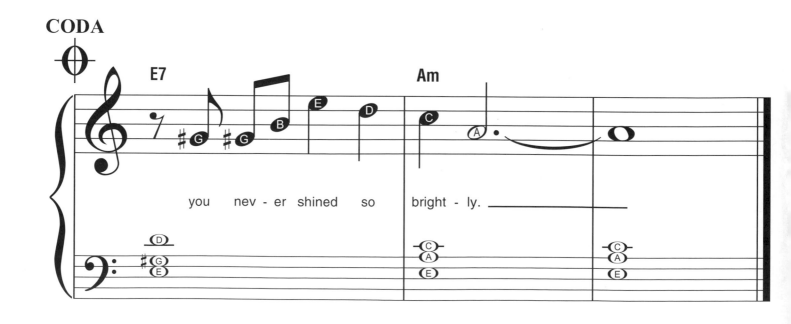

you nev - er shined so   bright - ly. _____

Girls Like You

Words and Music by Adam Levine,
Brittany Hazzard, Jason Evigan,
Gian Stone and Henry Walter

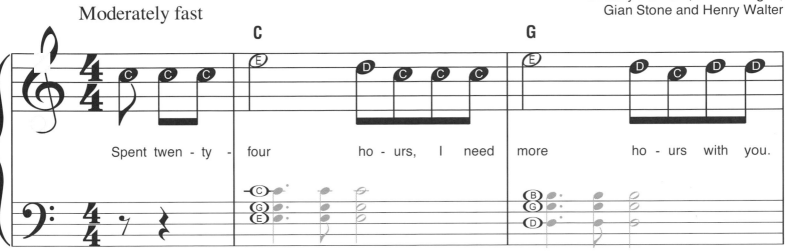

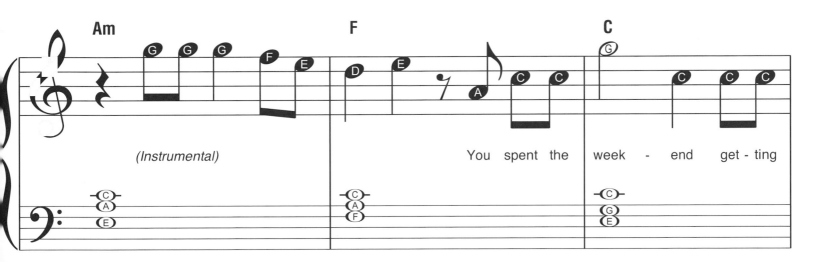

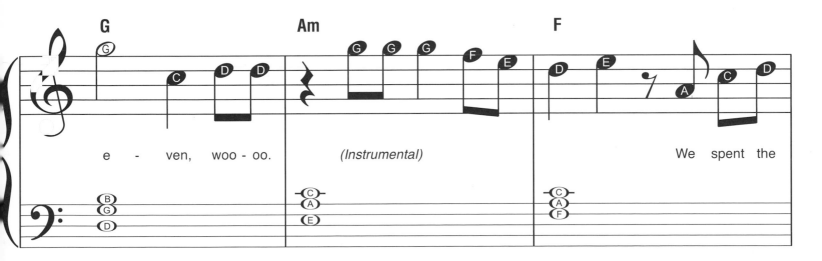

22

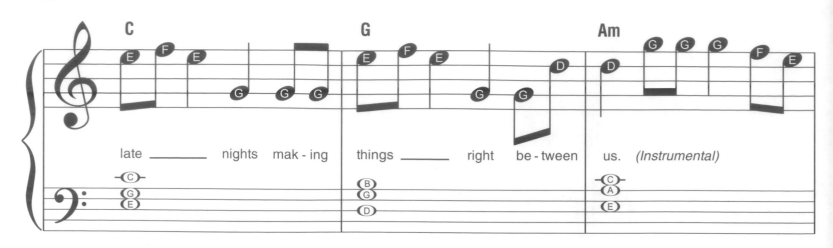

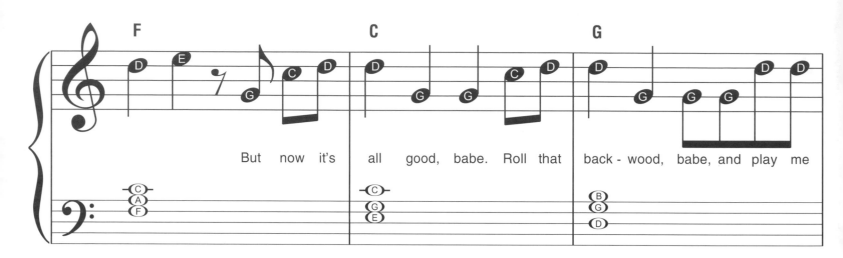

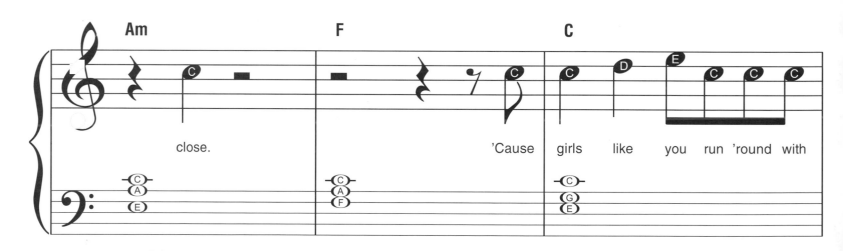

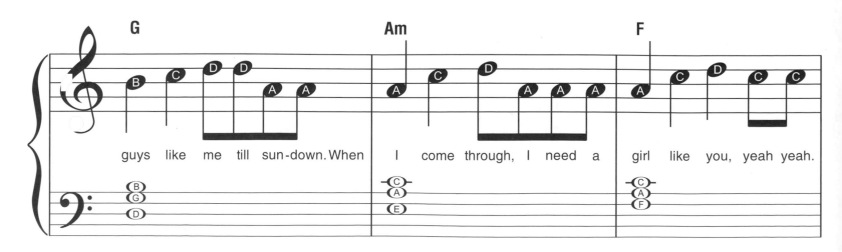

23

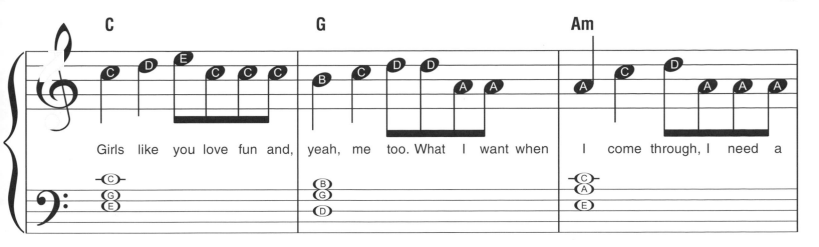

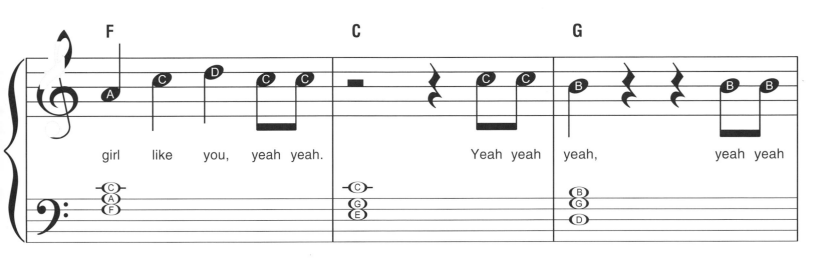

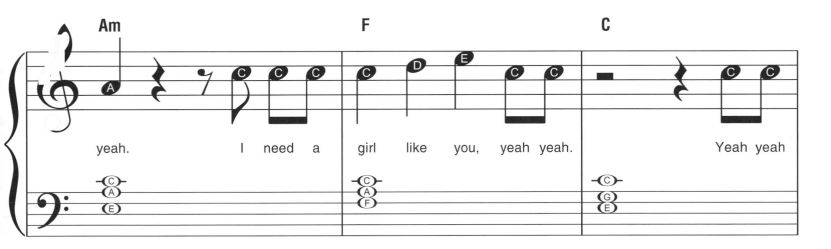

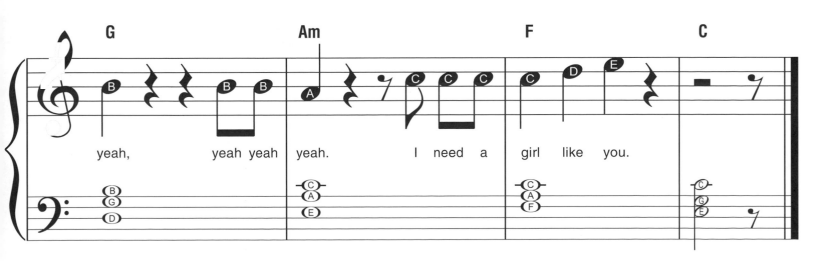

Happier

Words and Music by Marshmello,
Steve Mac and Dan Smith

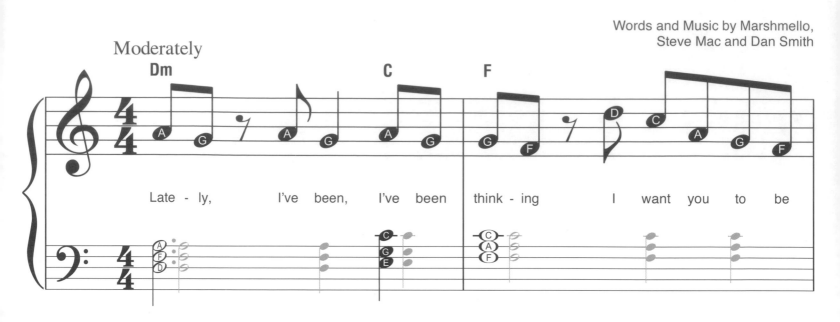

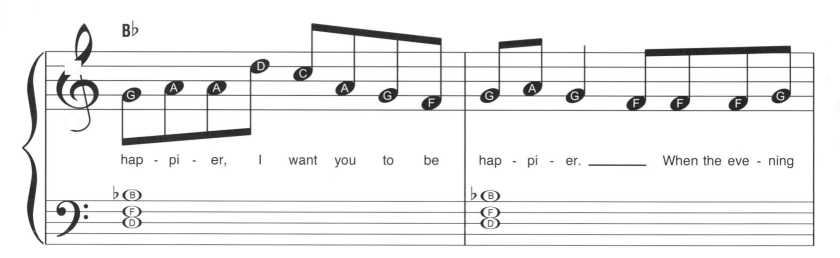

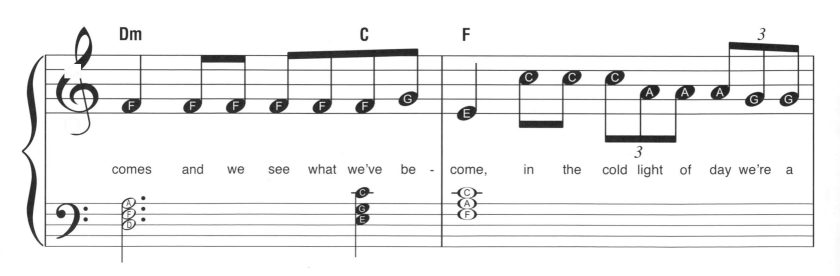

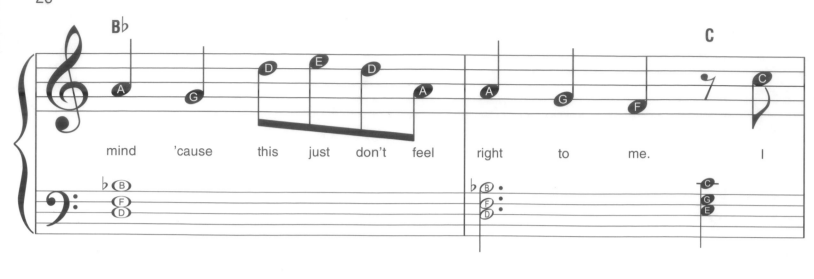

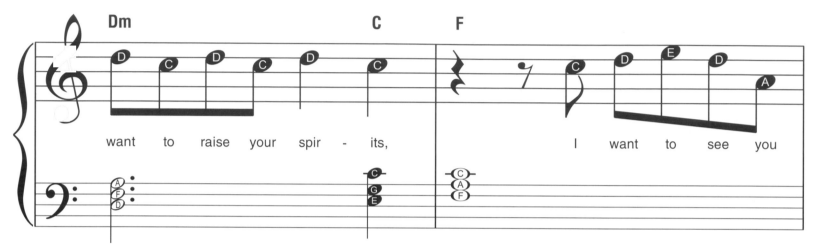

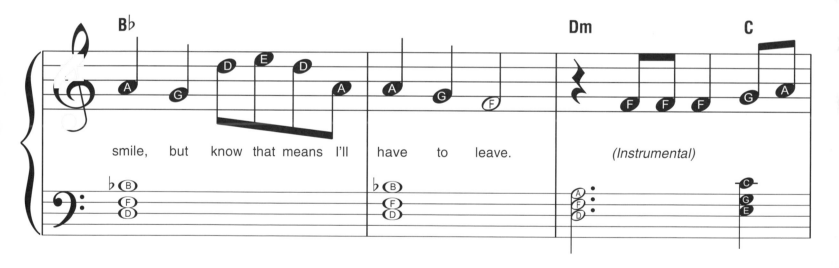

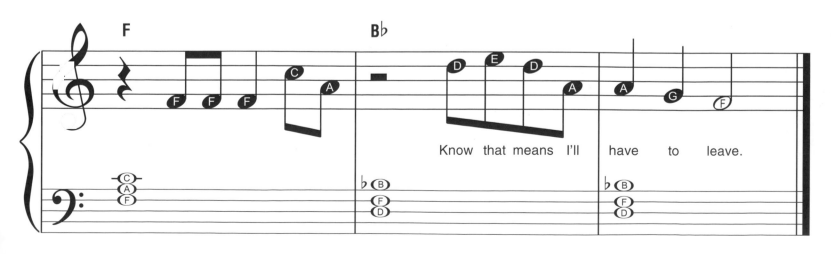

Happy
from DESPICABLE ME 2

Words and Music by
Pharrell Williams

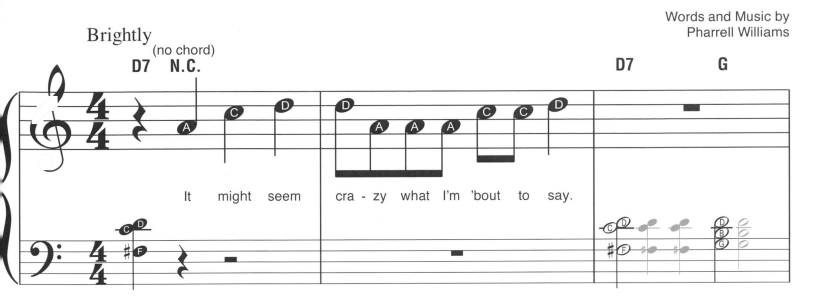

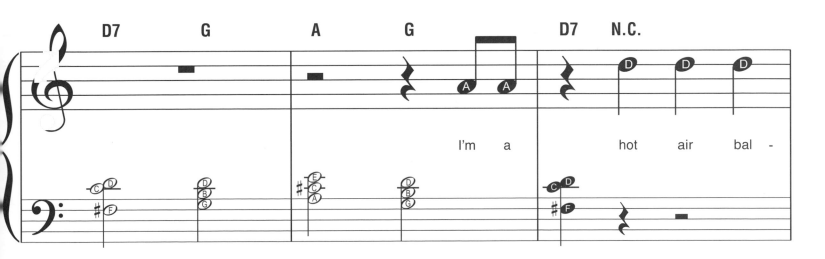

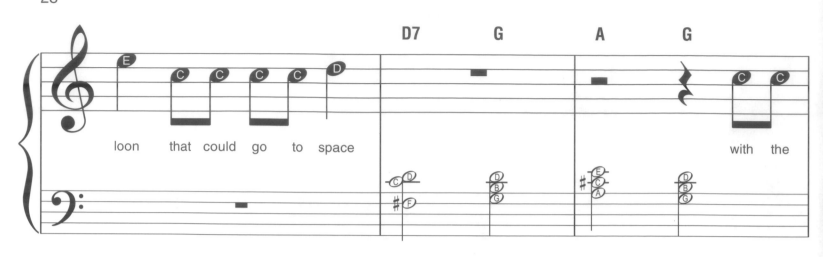

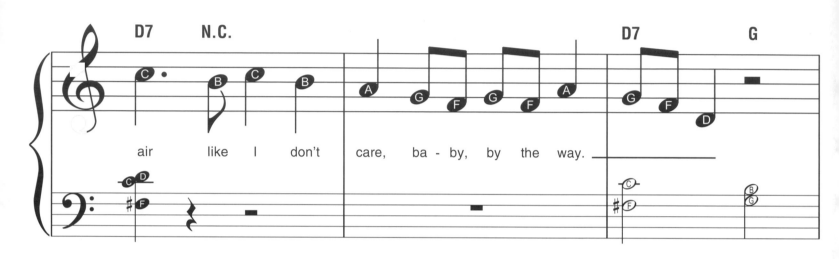

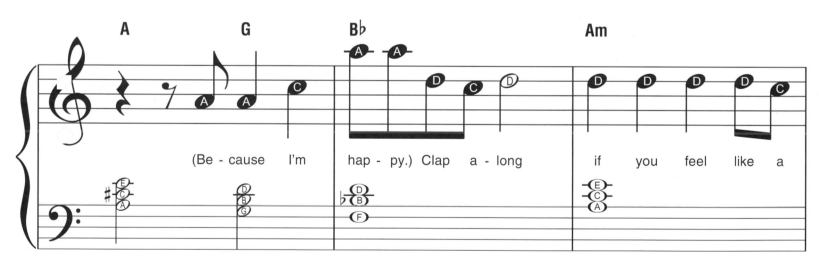

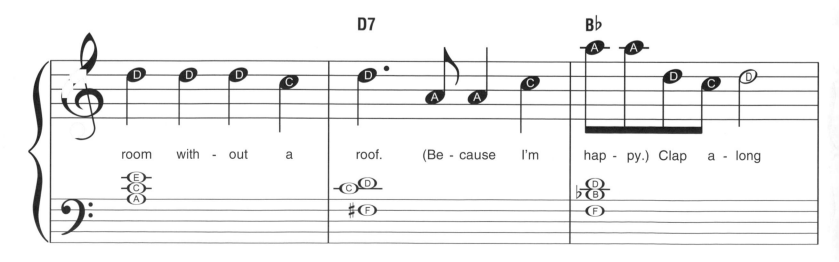

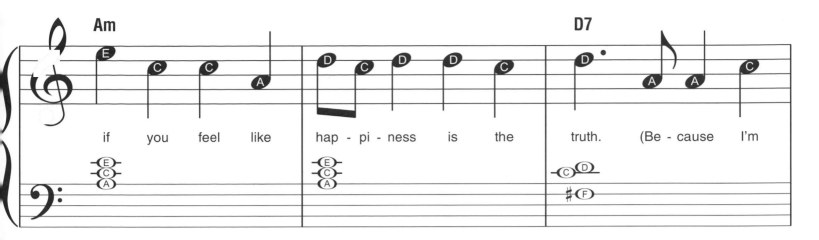

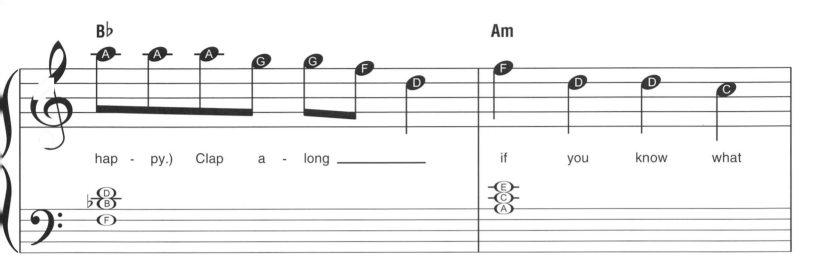

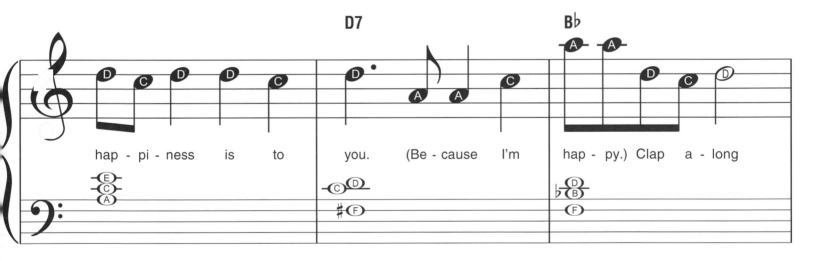

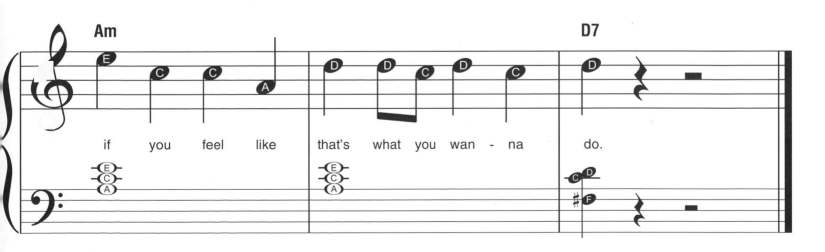

Hey, Soul Sister

Words and Music by Pat Monahan,
Espen Lind and Amund Bjørklund

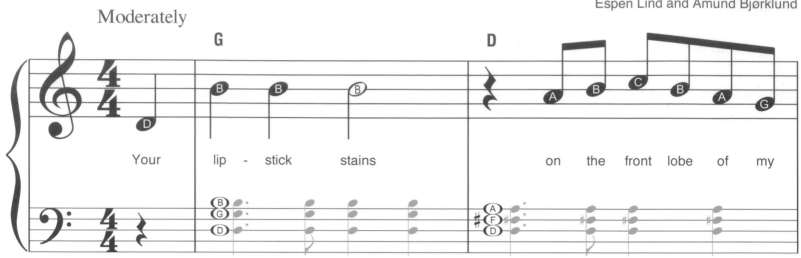

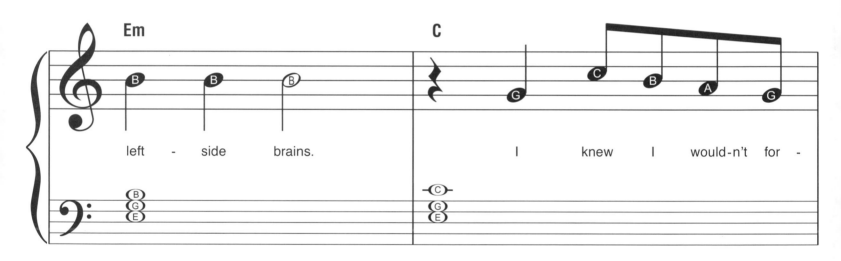

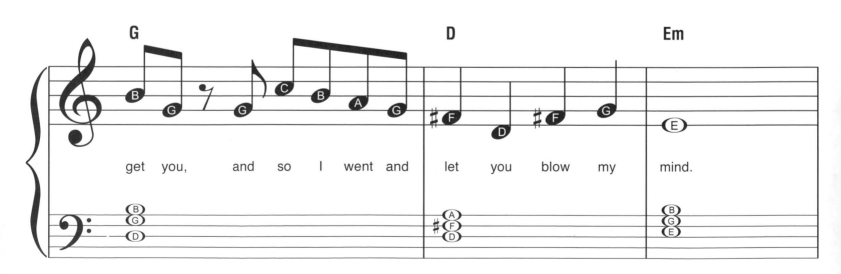

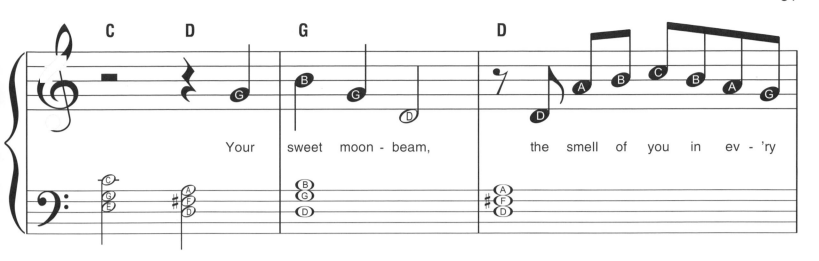

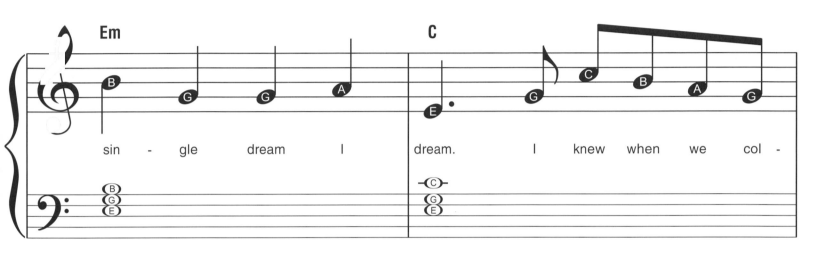

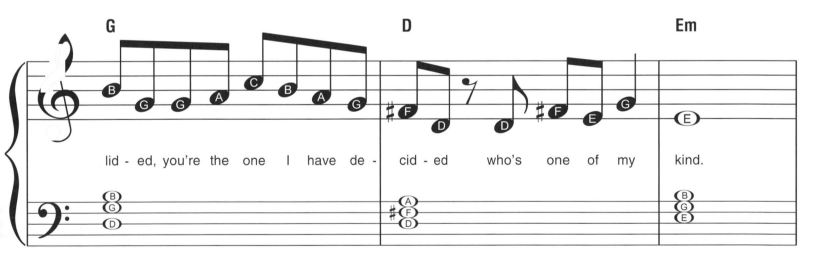

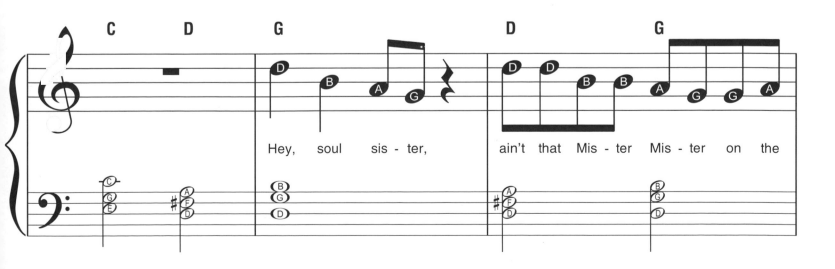

High Hopes

Words and Music by Brendon Urie,
Samuel Hollander, William Lobban Bean,
Jonas Jeberg, Jacob Sinclair,
Jenny Owen Youngs, Ilsey Juber,
Lauren Pritchard and Tayla Parx

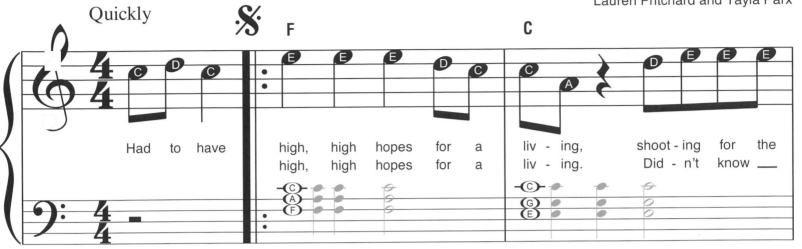

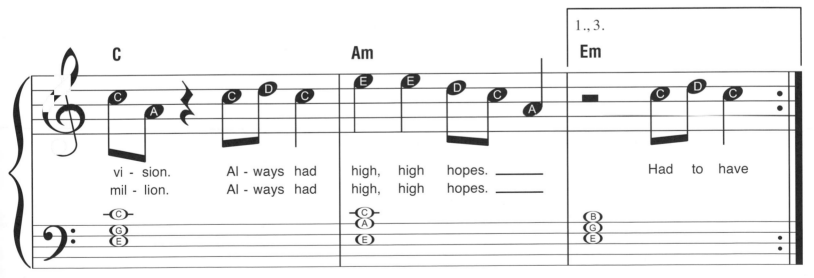

34

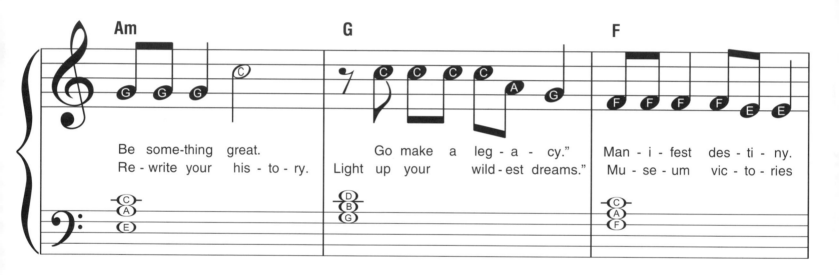

2.
(no chord)

ev - 'ry - thing. Ma - ma said, "Don't give up. It's a

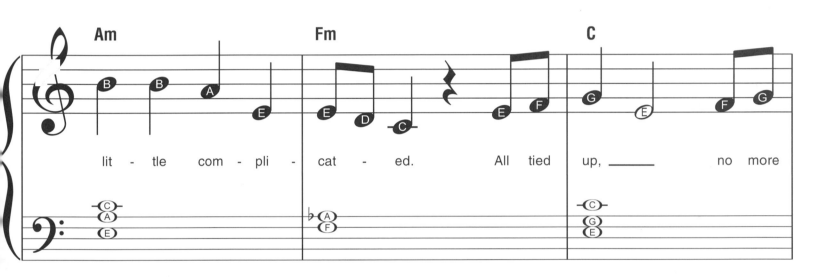

lit - tle com - pli - cat - ed. All tied up, _____ no more

D.S. al Fine
(Return to 𝄌
and play to Fine)

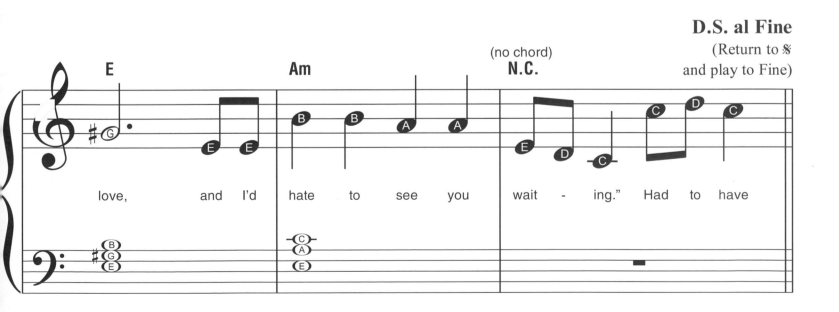

love, and I'd hate to see you wait - ing." Had to have

How Far I'll Go
from MOANA

Music and Lyrics by
Lin-Manuel Miranda

Moderately

I've been star - ing at the edge of the wa - ter long

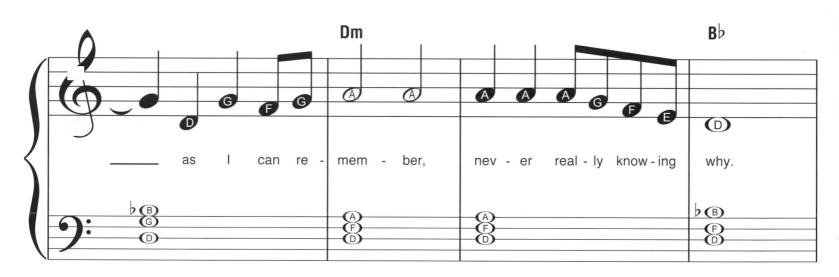

___ as I can re - mem - ber, nev - er real - ly know - ing why.

I wish I could be the per - fect daugh - ter,

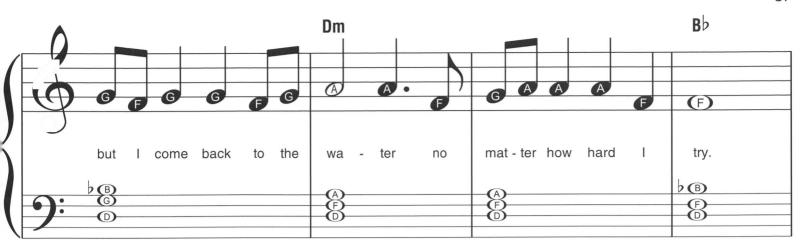

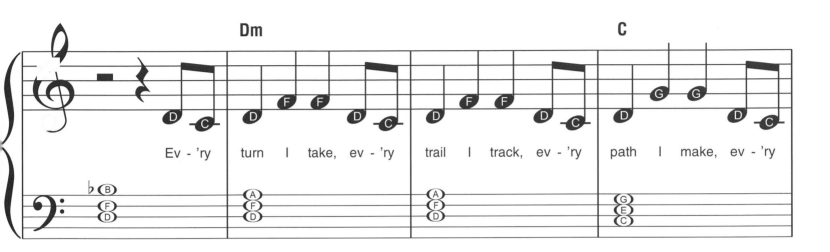

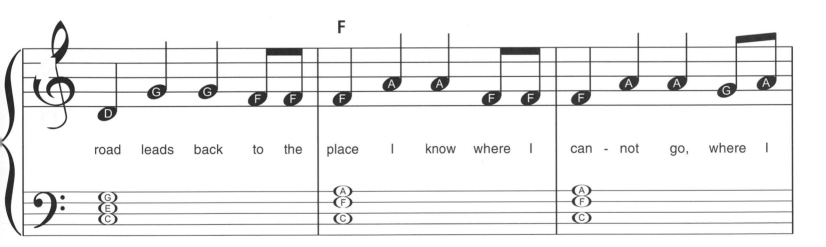

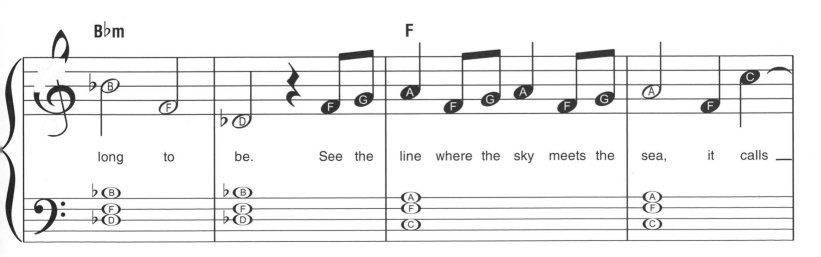

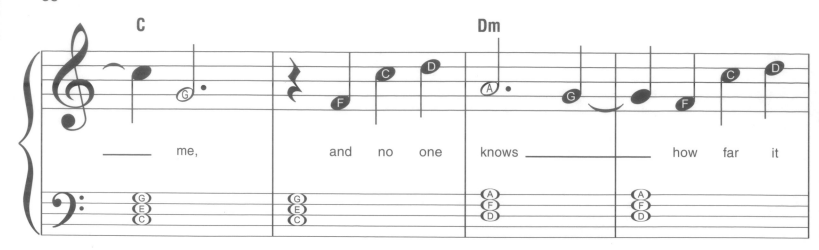

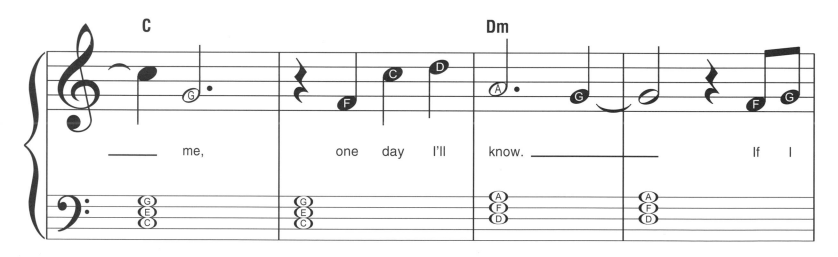

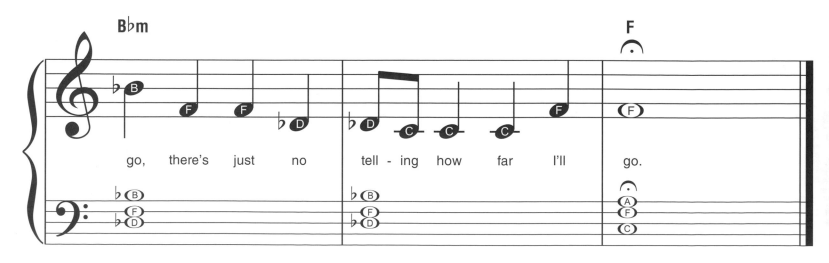

Just Give Me a Reason

Words and Music by Alecia Moore,
Jeff Bhasker and Nate Ruess

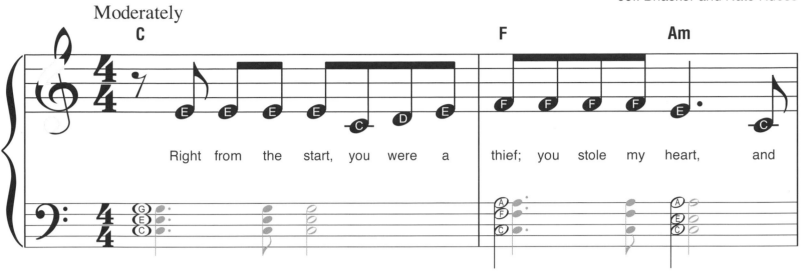

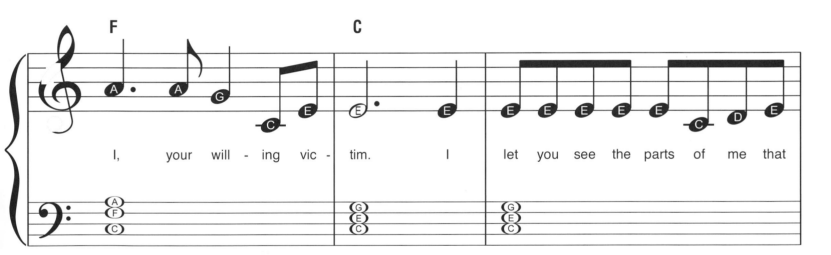

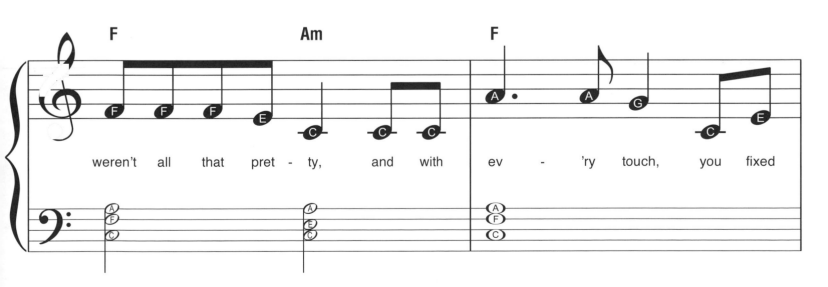

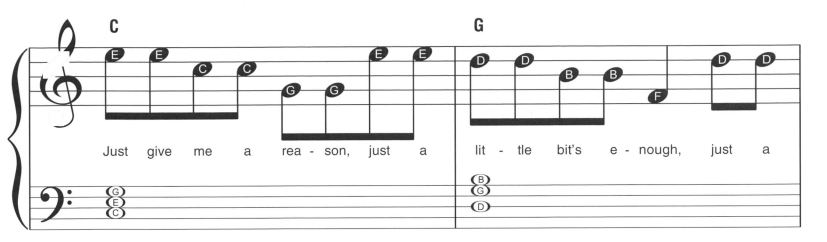

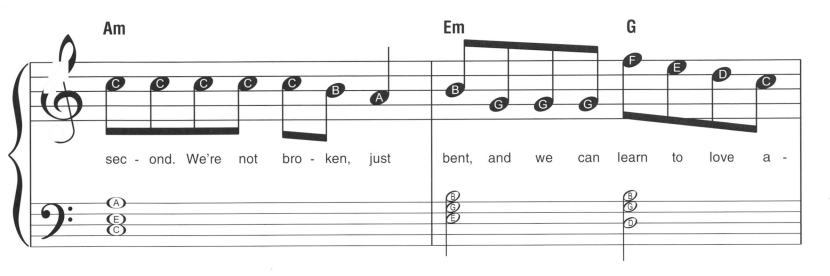

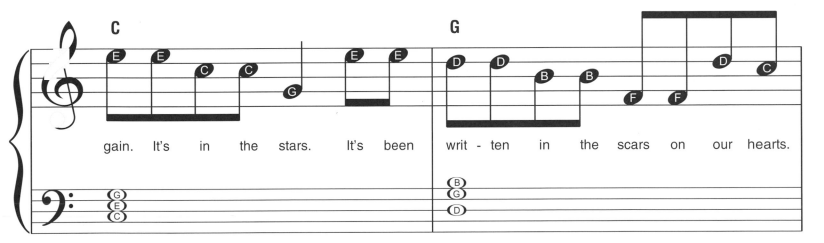

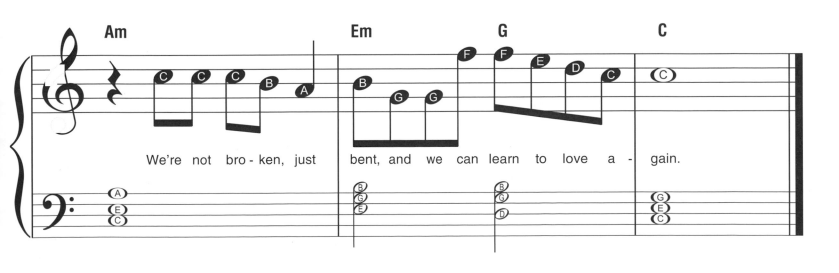

Just the Way You Are

Words and Music by Bruno Mars,
Ari Levine, Philip Lawrence,
Khari Cain and Khalil Walton

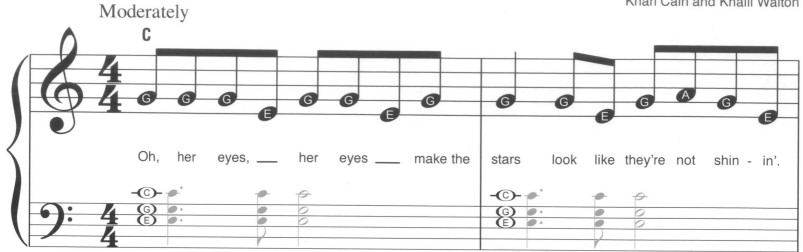

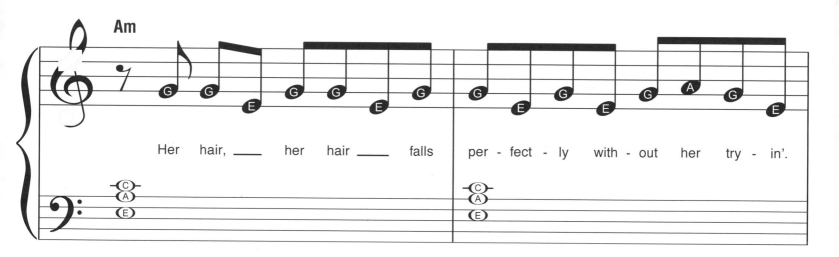

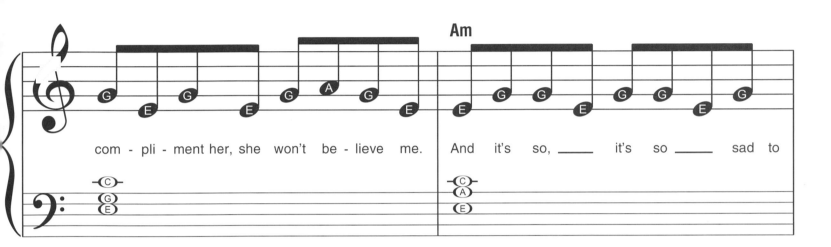

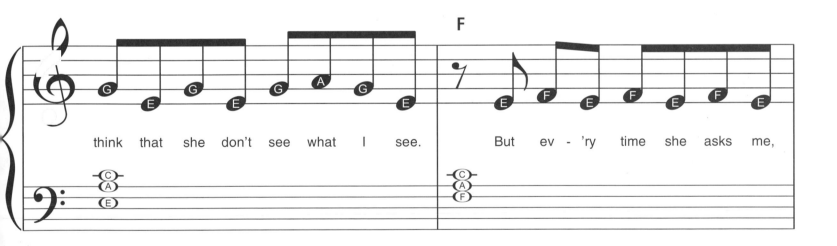

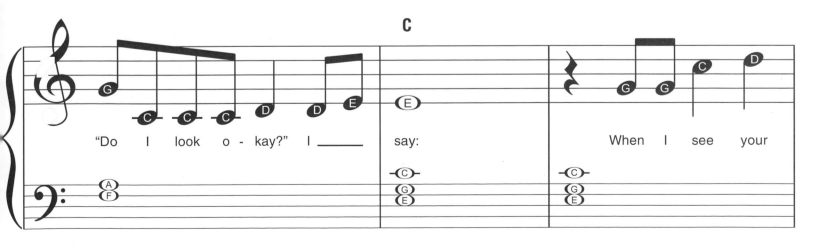

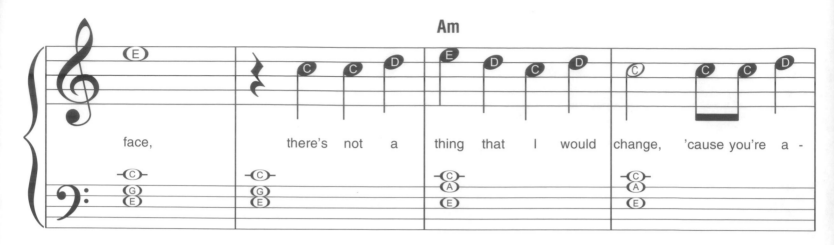

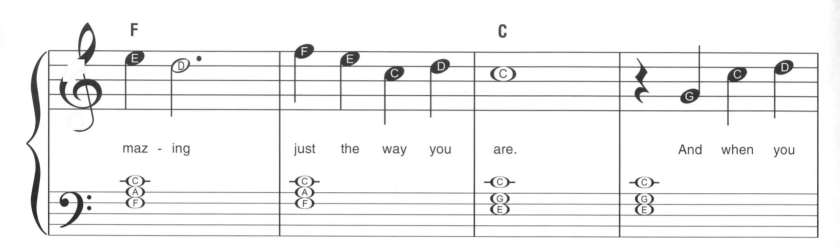

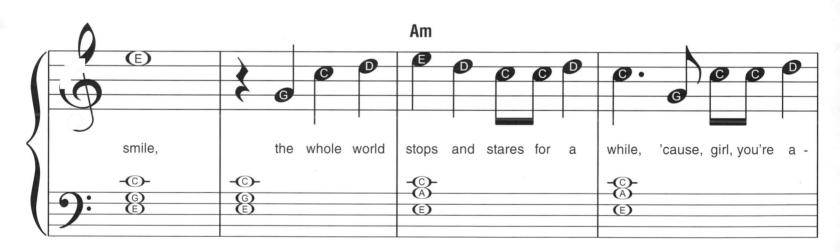

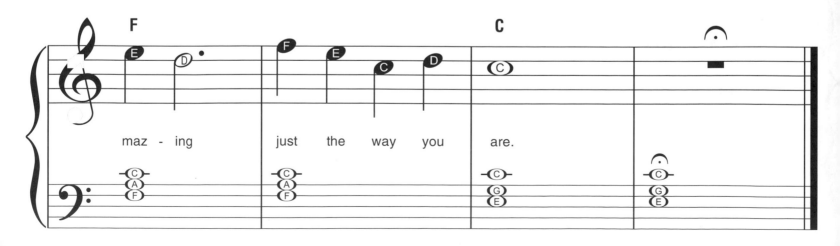

Let Her Go

Words and Music by
Michael David Rosenberg

Well, you on - ly need the light when it's burn - in' low.
high when you're feel - in' low. On - ly miss the
On - ly hate the

sun when it starts to snow. On - ly know you love her when you let her go.
road when you're miss - in' home.

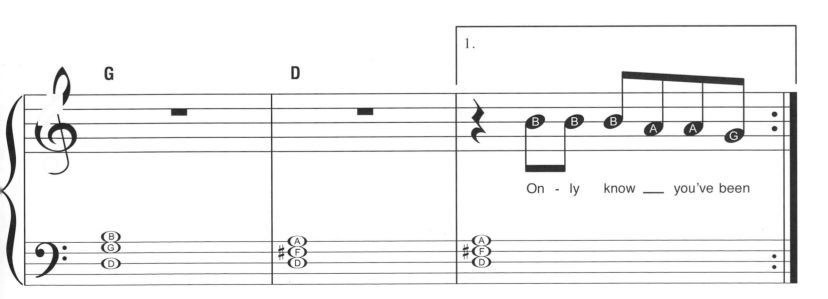

1.

On - ly know ___ you've been

46

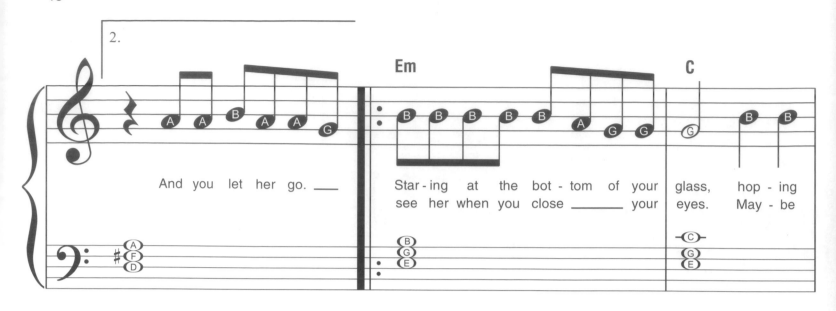

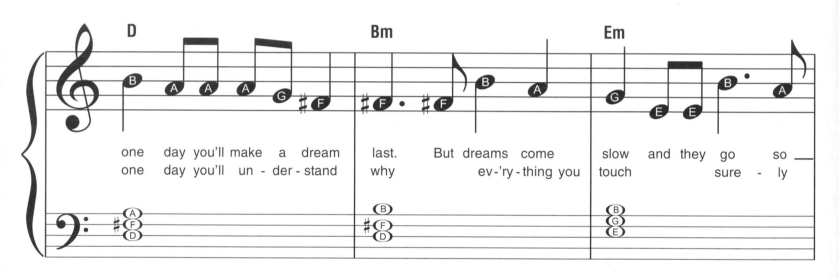

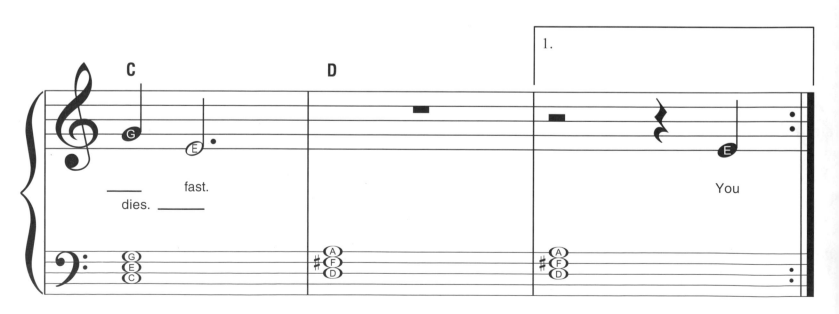

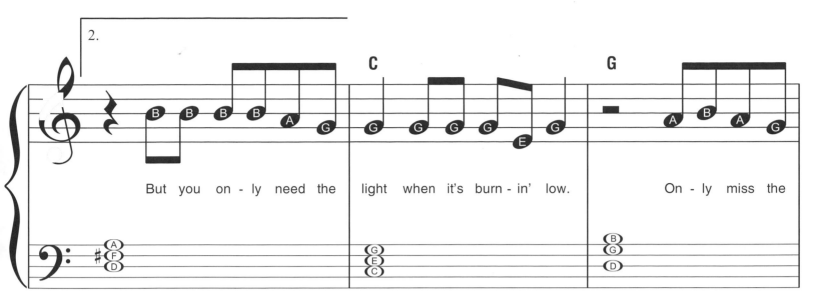

But you on - ly need the light when it's burn - in' low. On - ly miss the

sun when it starts to snow. On - ly know you love her when you let her go.

And you let her go.

Lovely

Words and Music by Billie Eilish O'Connell,
Finneas O'Connell and Khalid Robinson

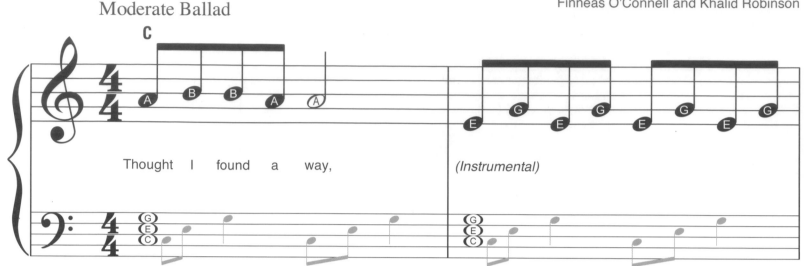

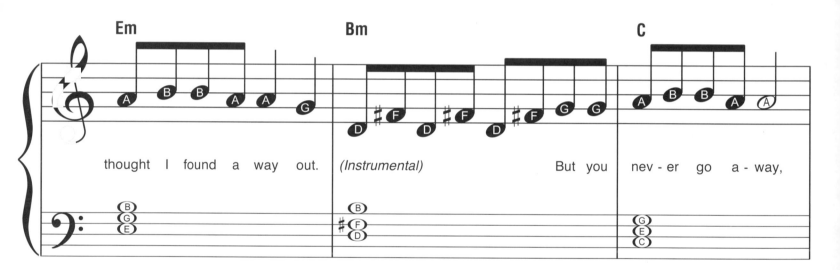

49

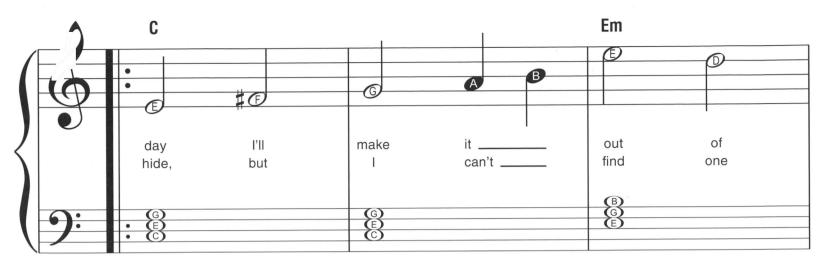

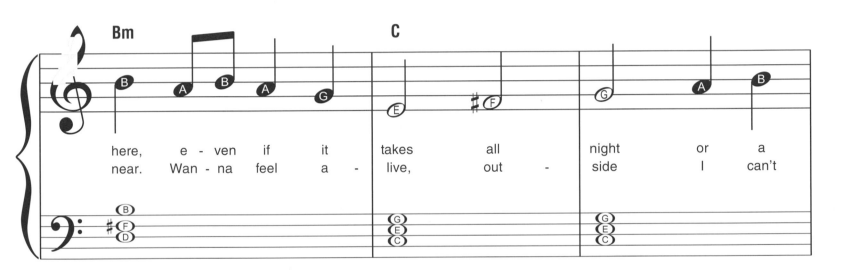

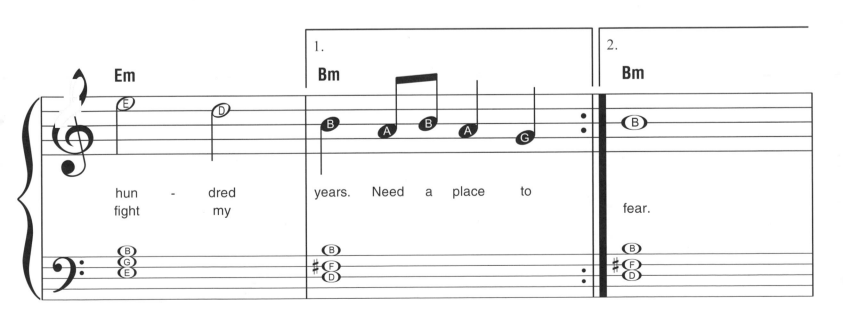

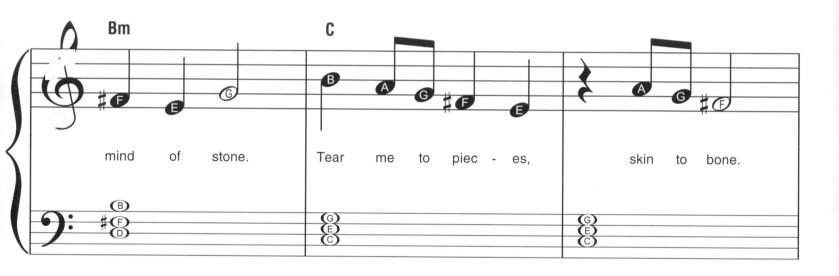

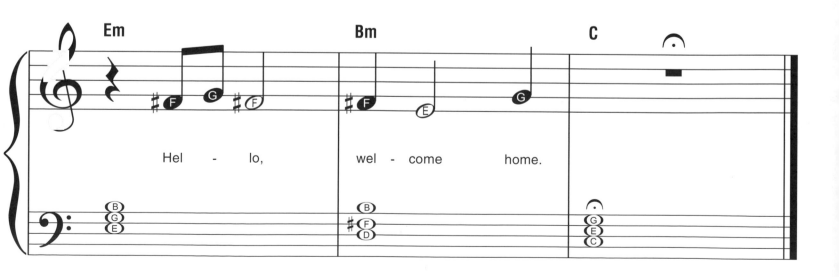

Old Town Road
(Remix)

Words and Music by Trent Reznor,
Billy Ray Cyrus, Jocelyn Donald,
Atticus Ross, Kiowa Roukema
and Montero Lamar Hill

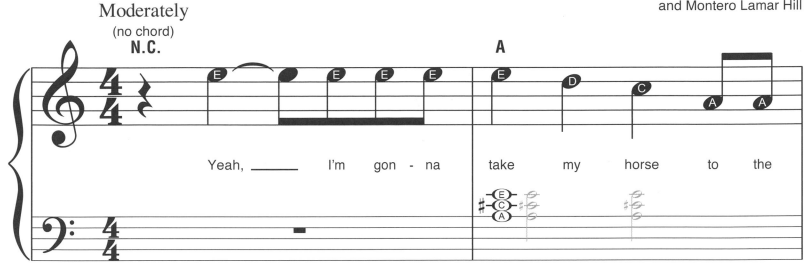

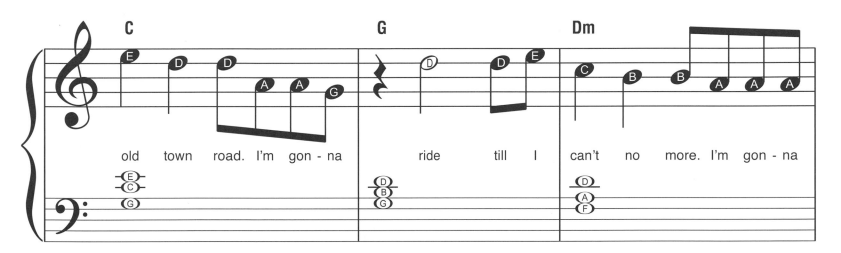

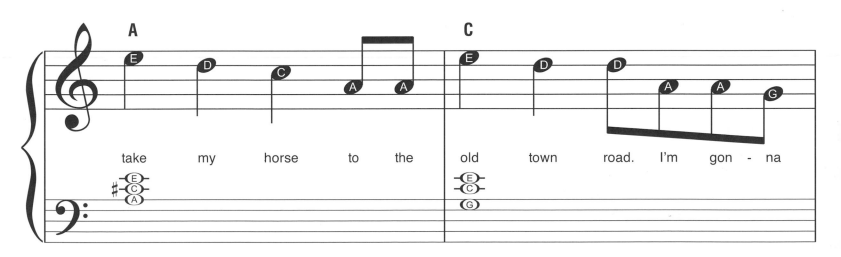

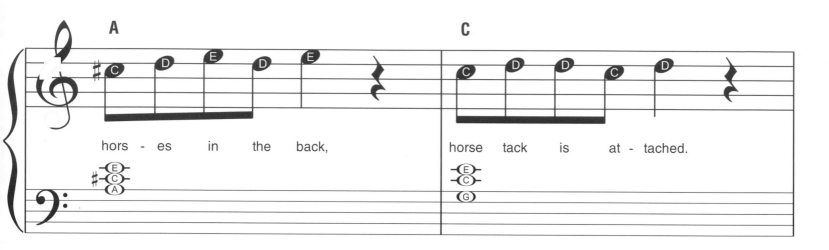

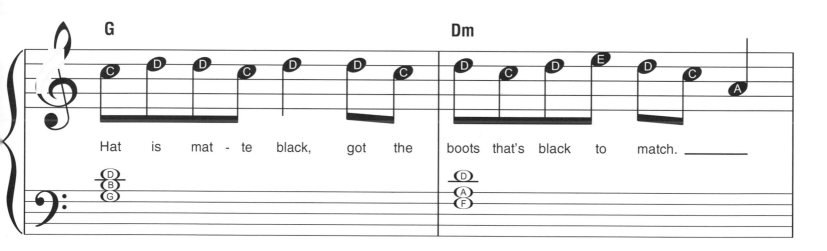

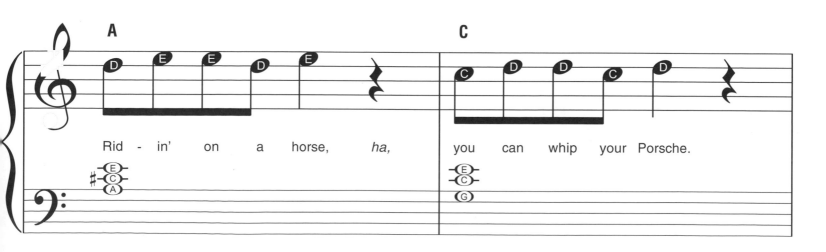

53

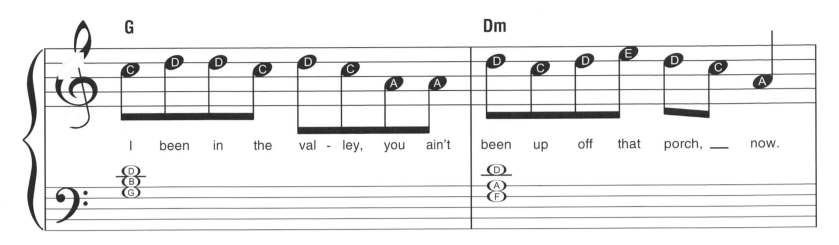

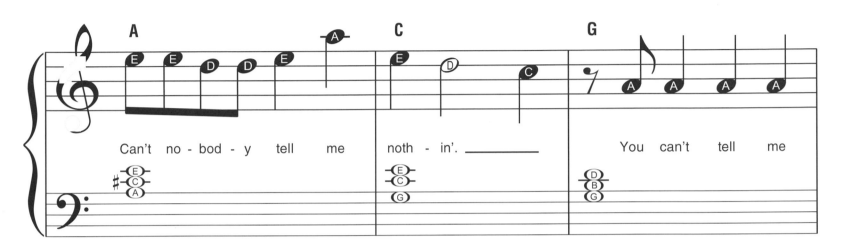

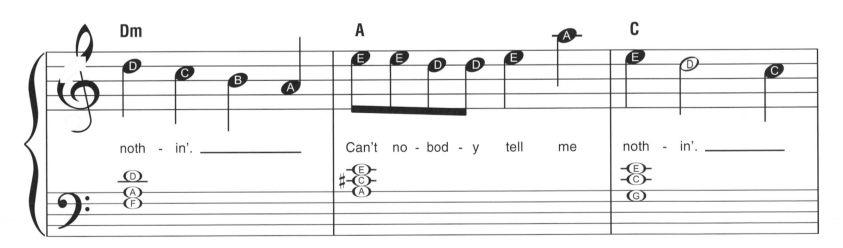

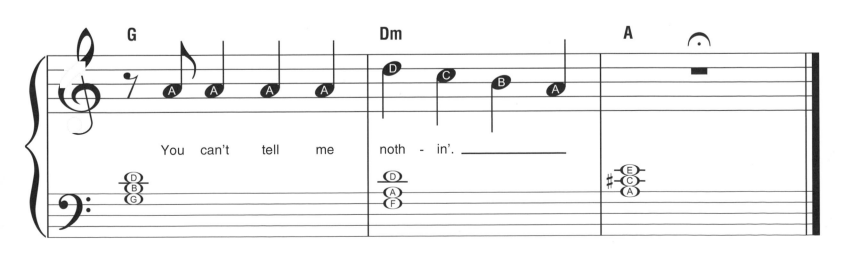

A Million Dreams
from THE GREATEST SHOWMAN

Words and Music by Benj Pasek
and Justin Paul

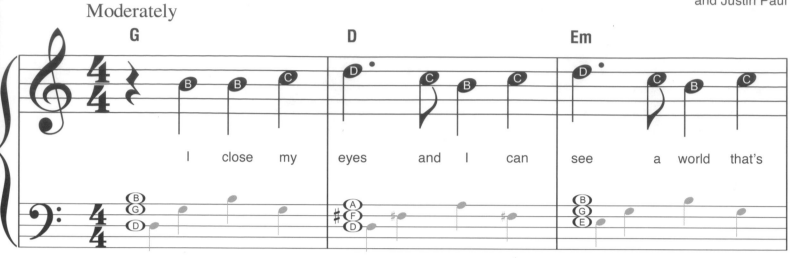

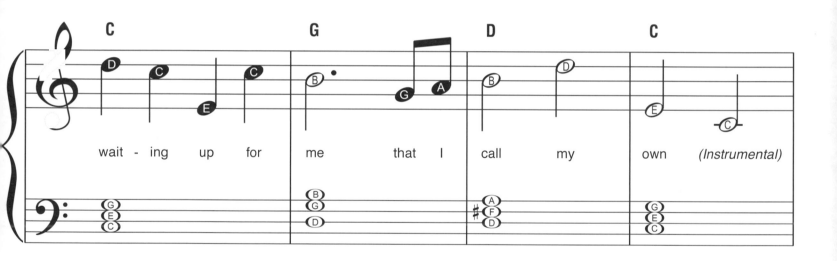

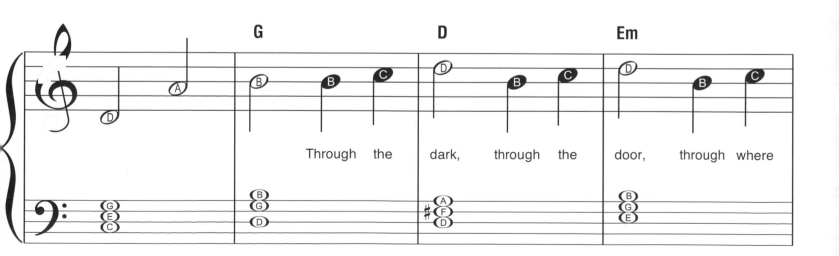

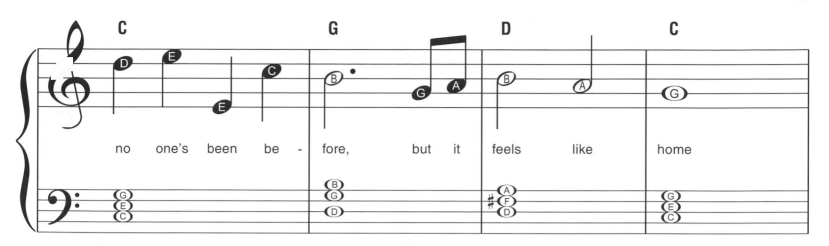

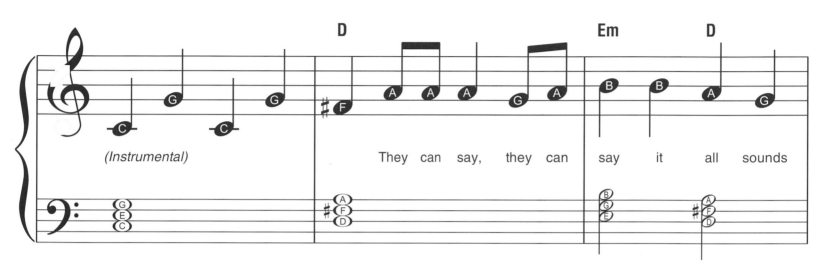

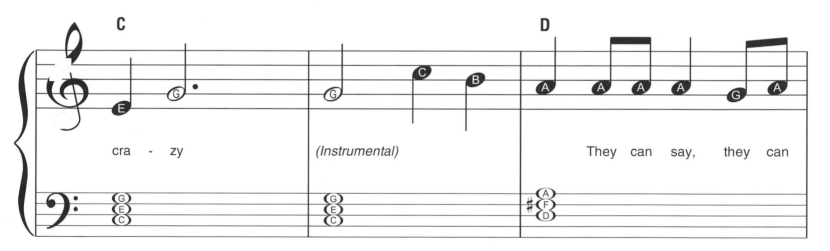

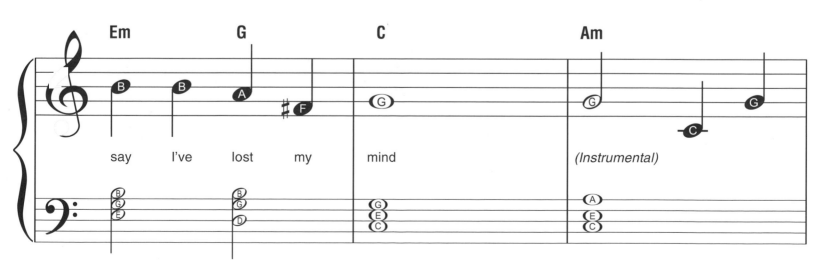

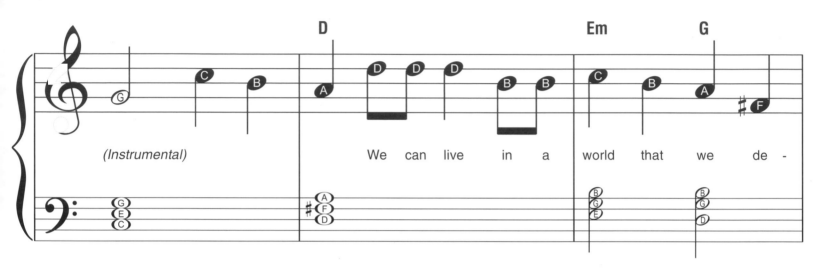

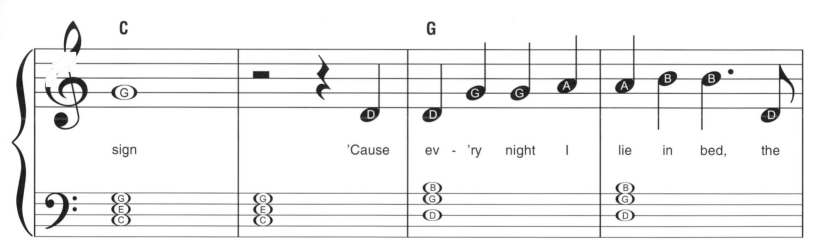

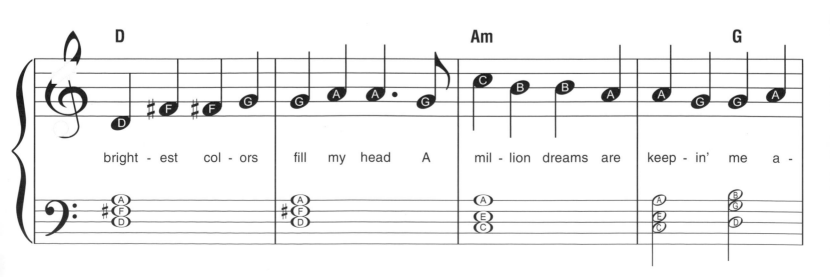

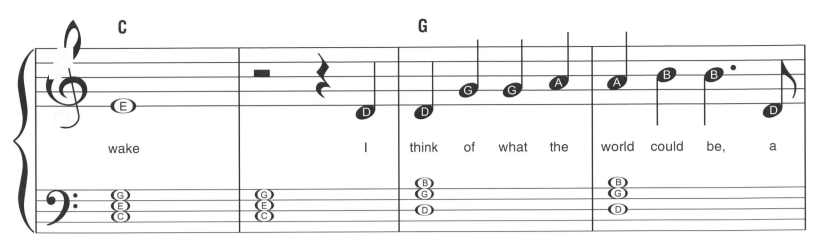

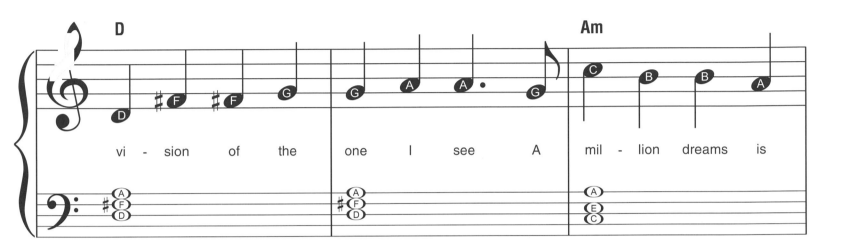

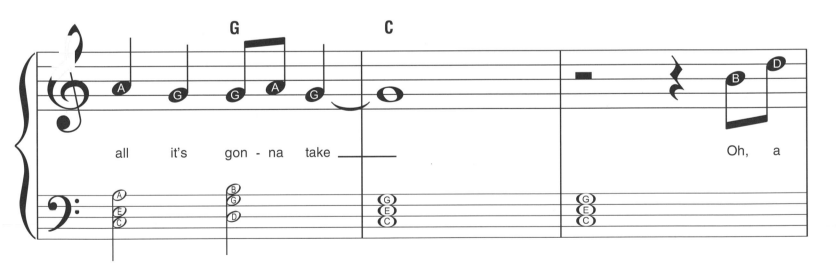

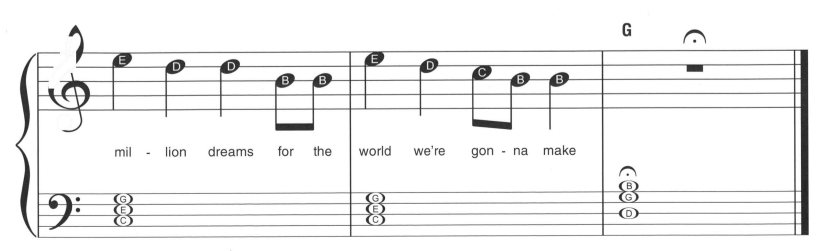

Rolling in the Deep

Words and Music by Adele Adkins
and Paul Epworth

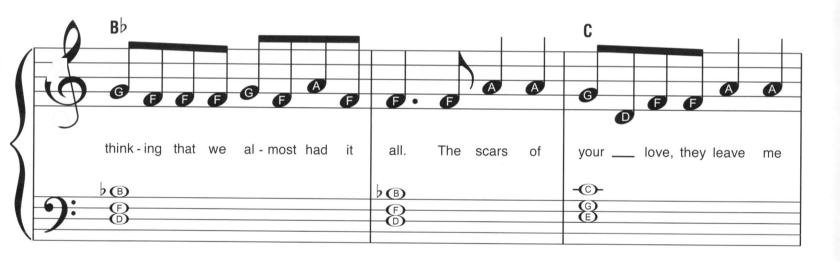

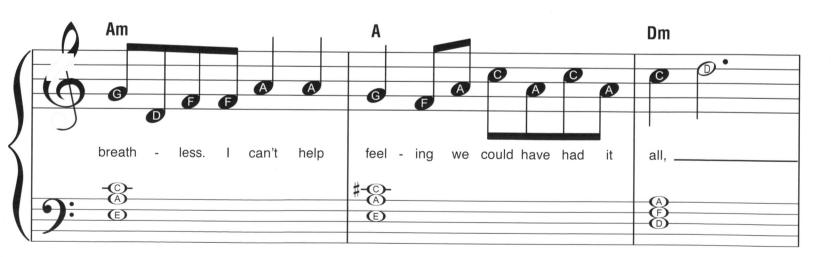

Shake It Off

Words and Music by Taylor Swift,
Max Martin and Shellback

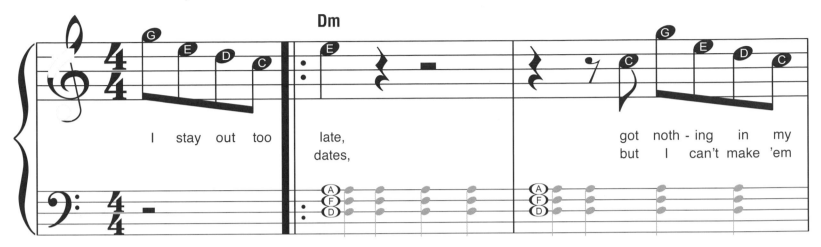

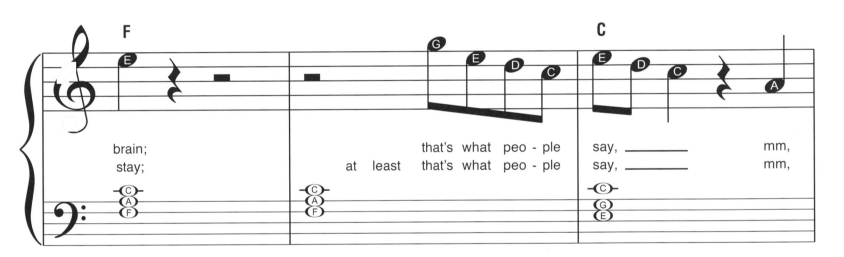

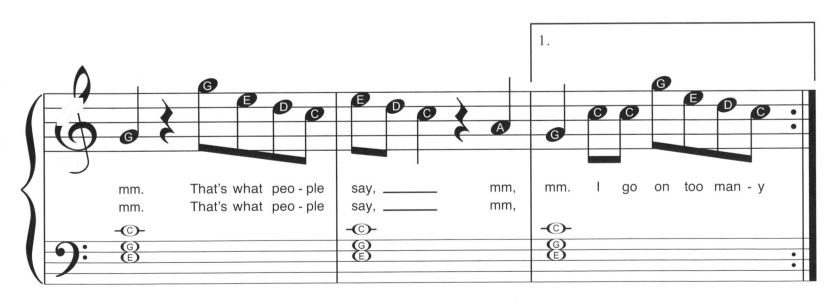

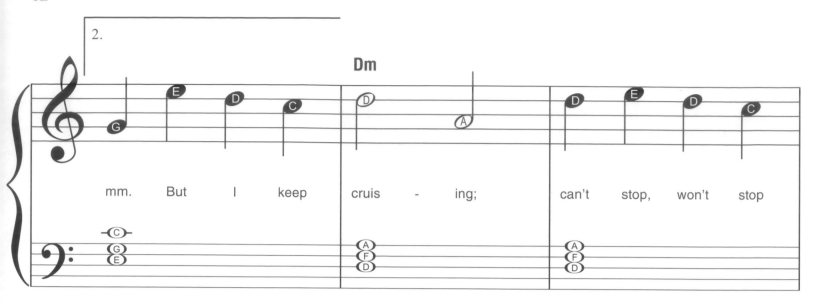

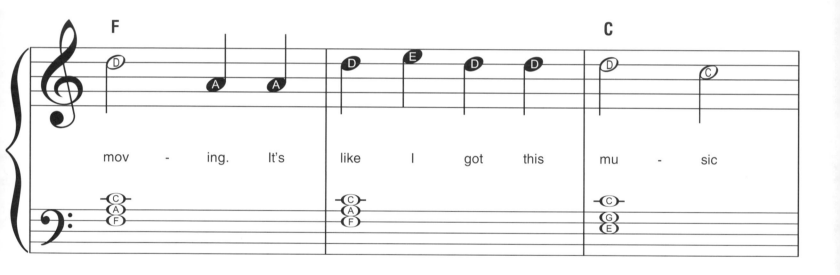

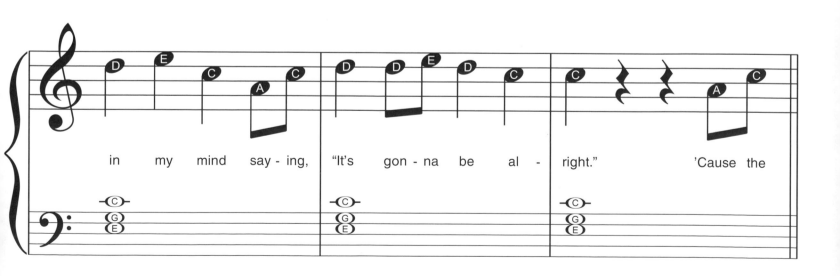

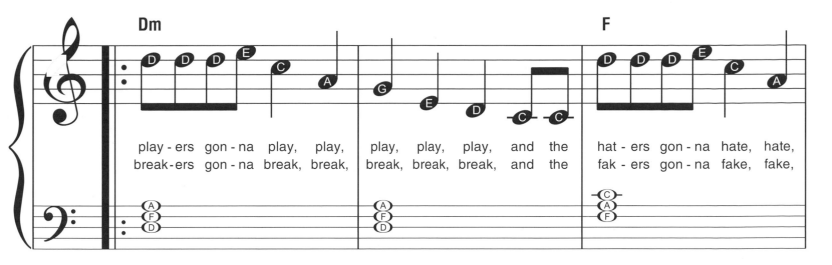

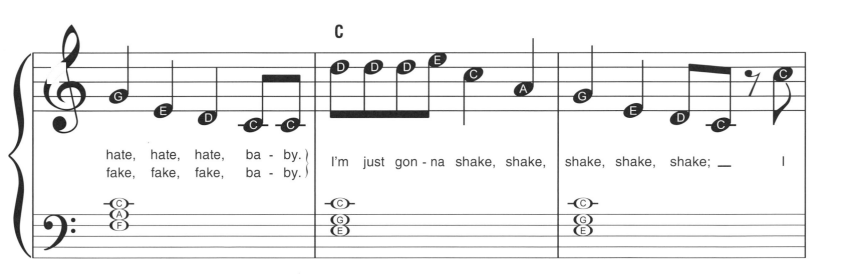

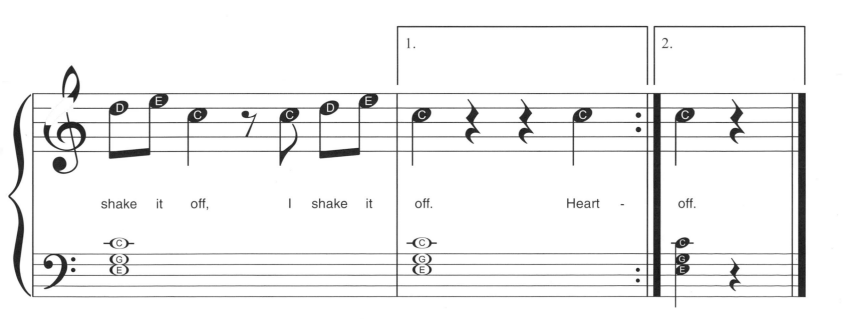

Shape of You

Words and Music by Ed Sheeran,
Kevin Briggs, Kandi Burruss,
Tameka Cottle, Steve Mac
and Johnny McDaid

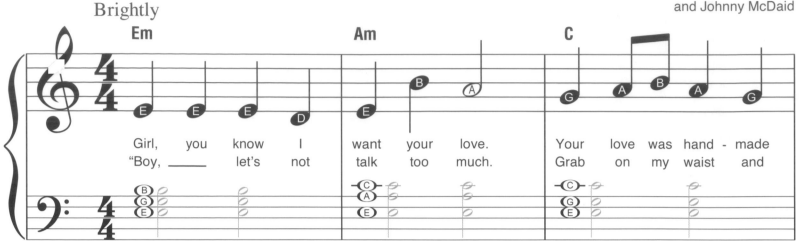

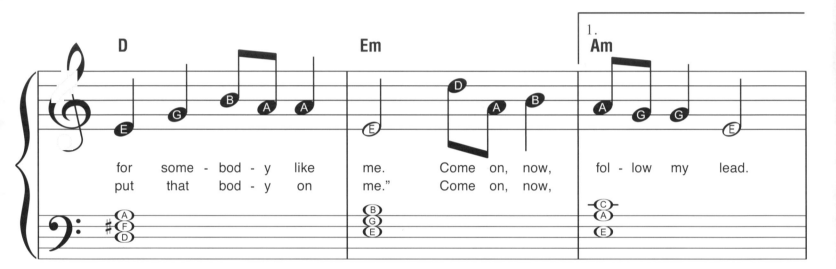

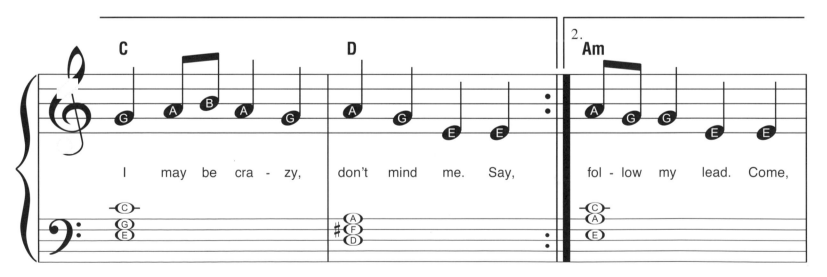

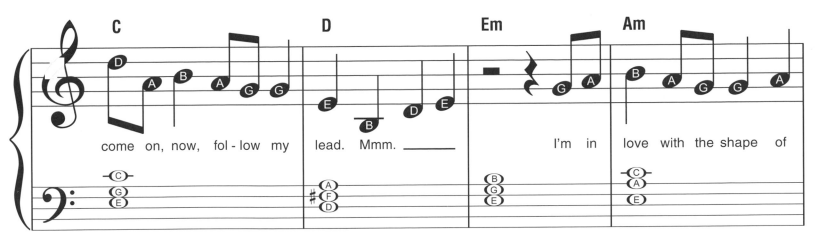

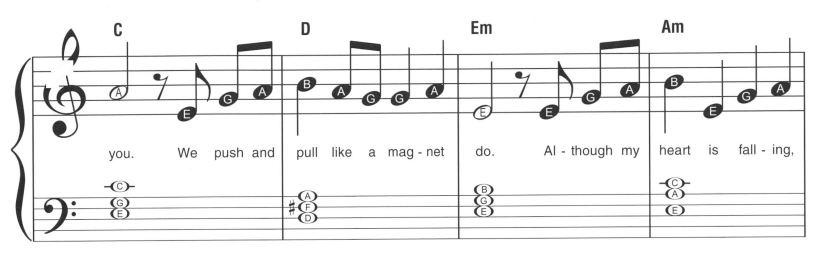

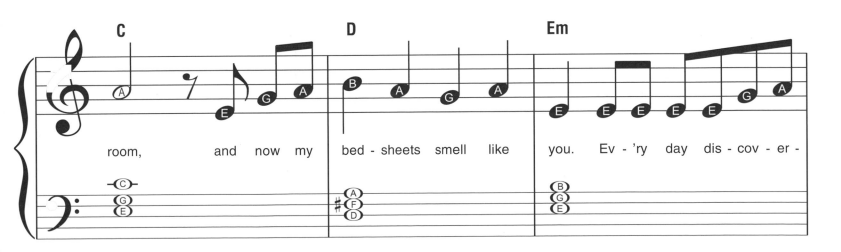

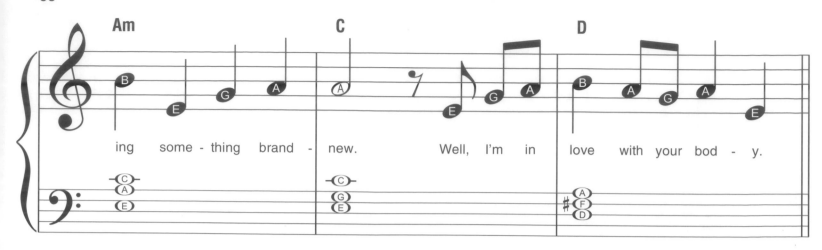

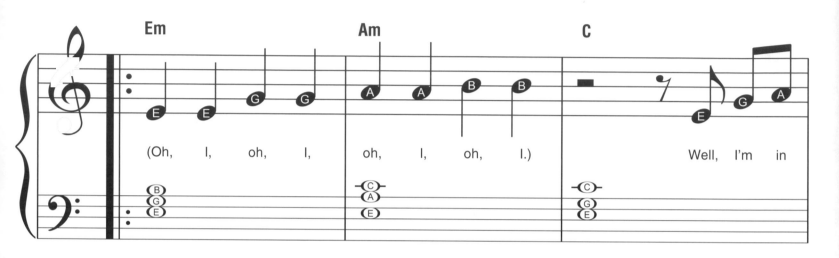

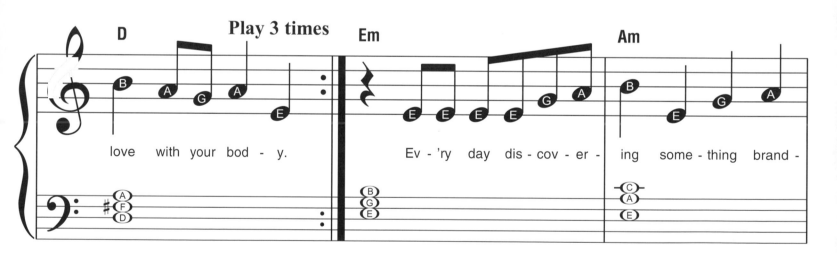

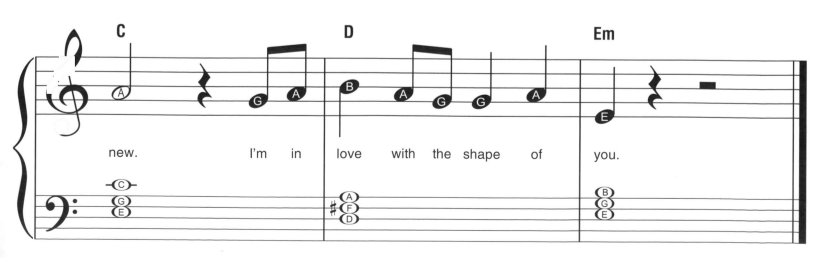

Shallow
from A STAR IS BORN

Words and Music by Stefani Germanotta,
Mark Ronson, Andrew Wyatt
and Anthony Rossomando

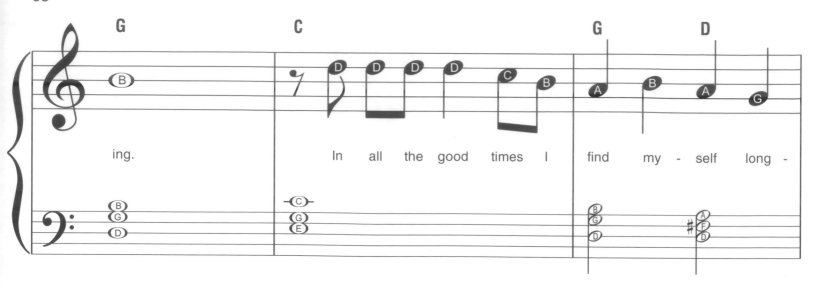

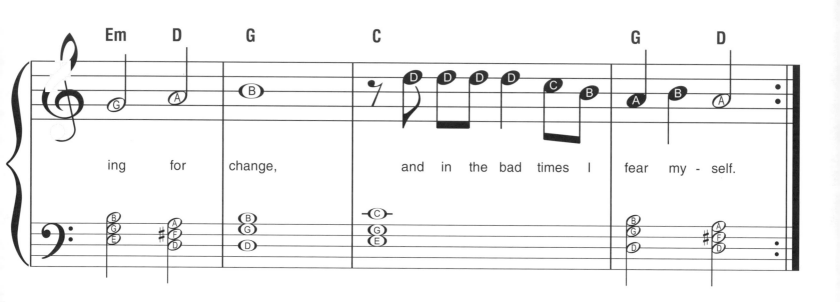

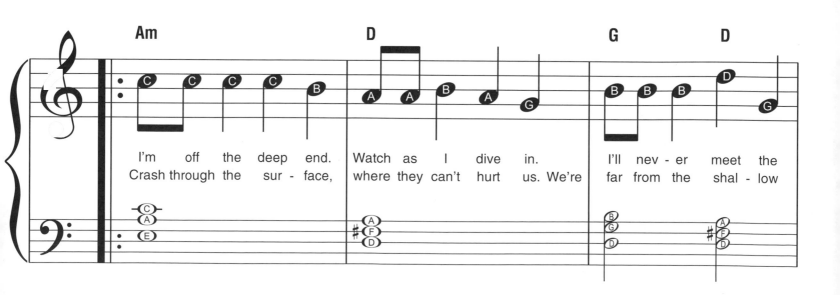

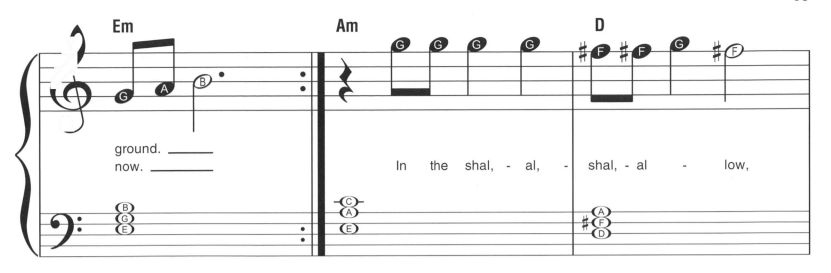

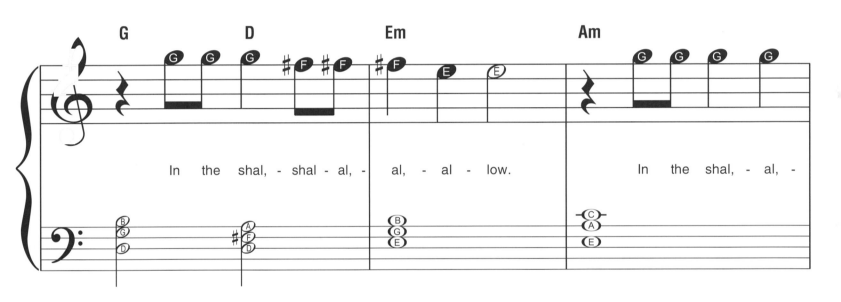

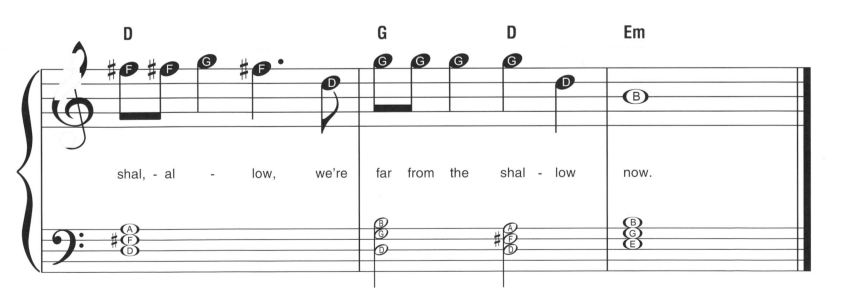

Some Nights

Words and Music by Jeff Bhasker,
Andrew Dost, Jack Antonoff
and Nate Ruess

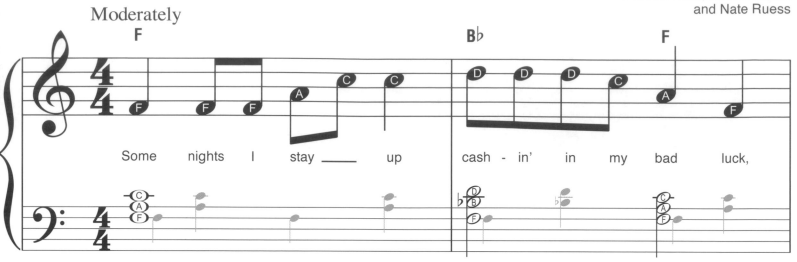

Some nights I stay ____ up cash - in' in my bad luck,

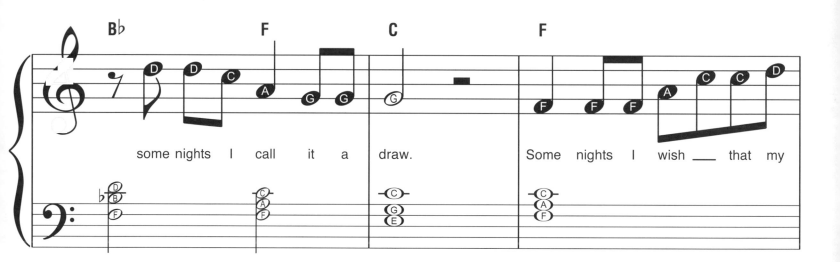

some nights I call it a draw. Some nights I wish ____ that my

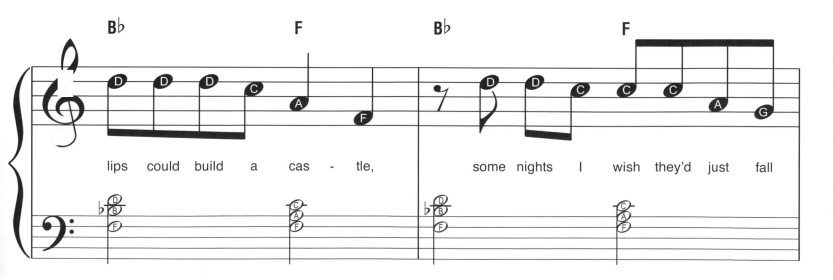

lips could build a cas - tle, some nights I wish they'd just fall

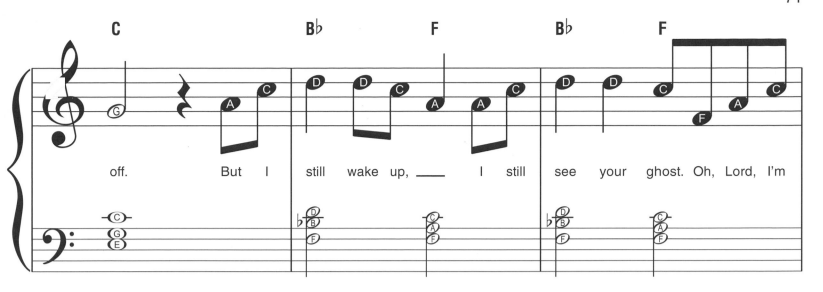

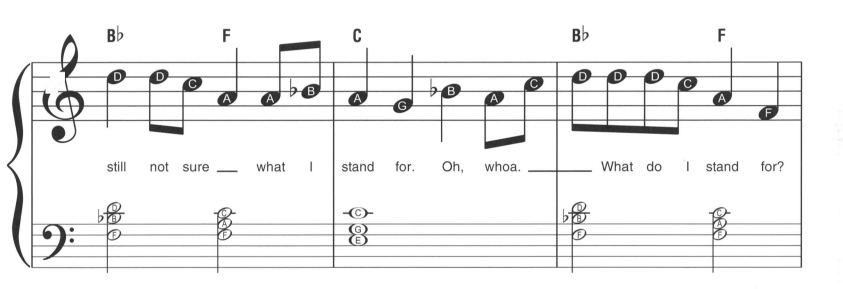

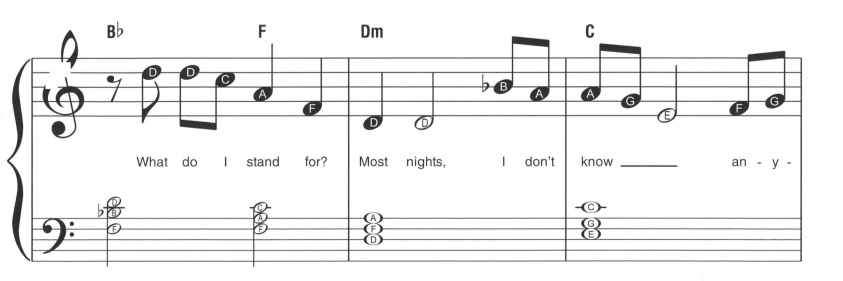

72

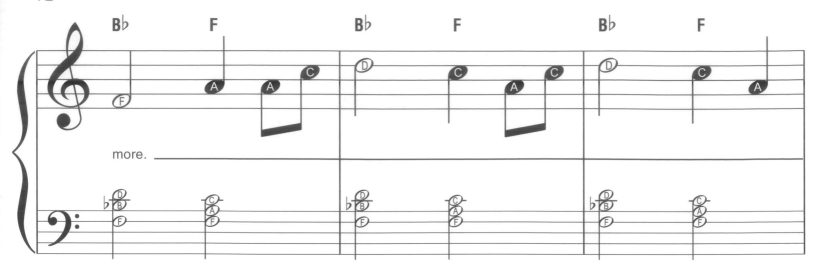

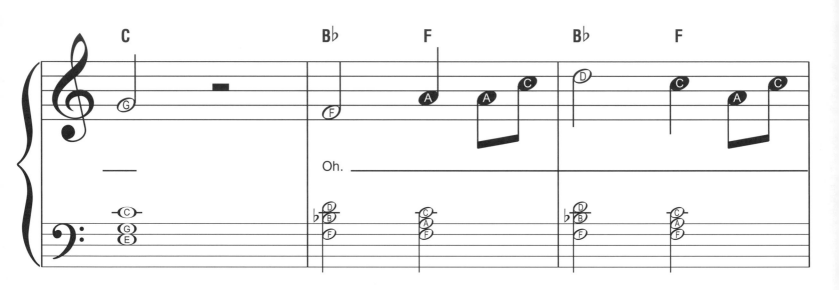

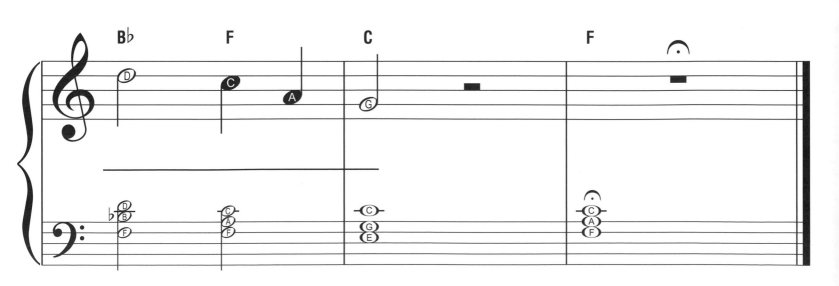

Someone You Loved

Words and Music by Lewis Capaldi,
Benjamin Kohn, Peter Kelleher,
Thomas Barnes and Samuel Roman

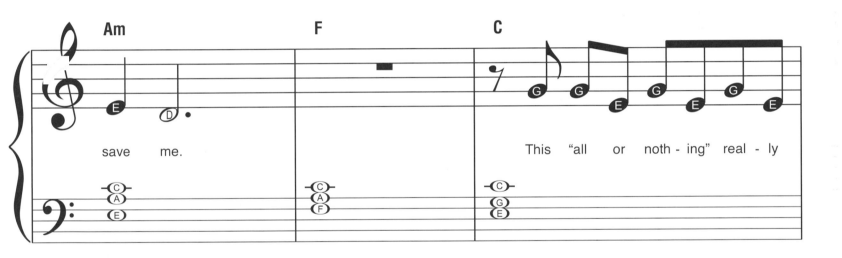

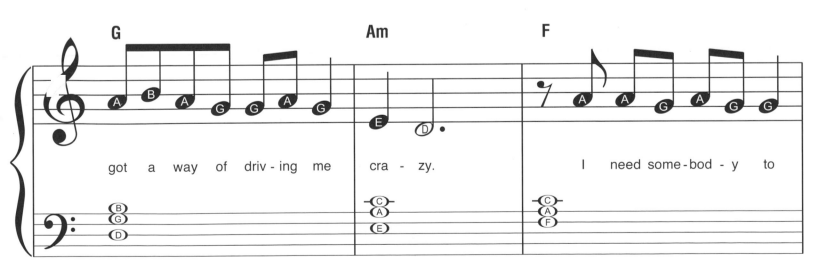

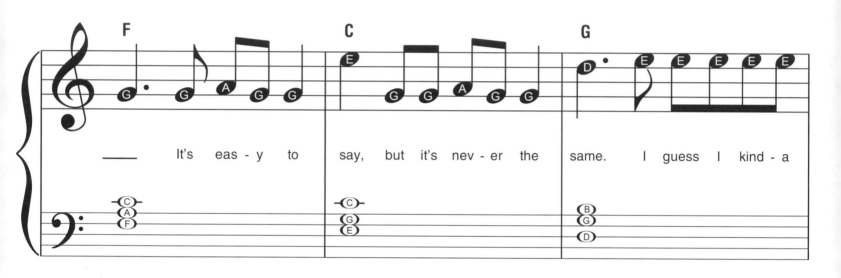

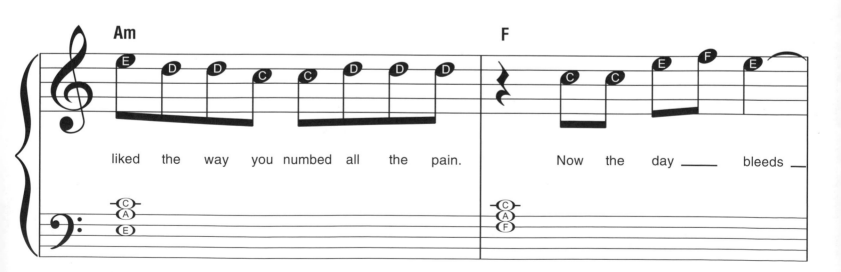

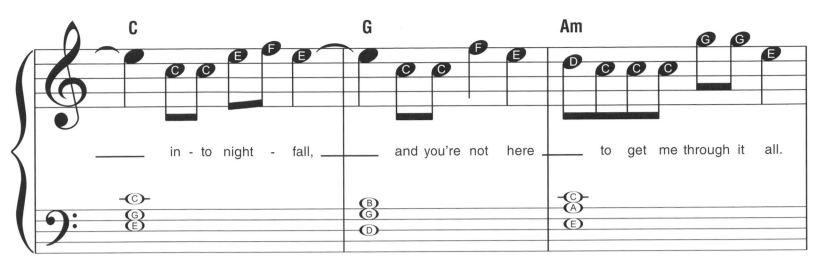

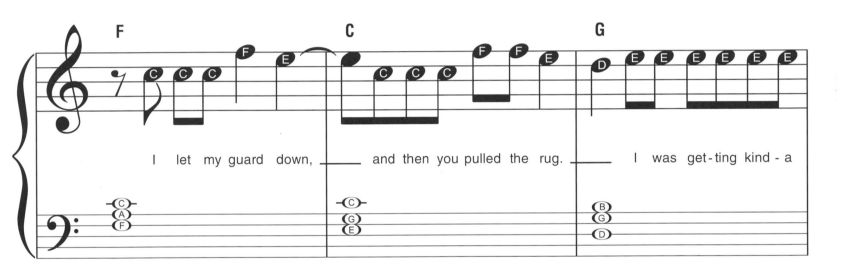

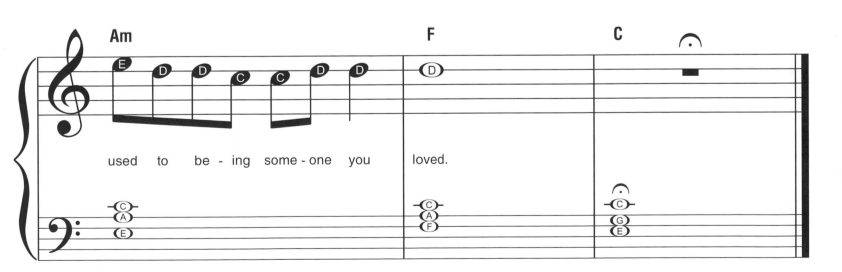

Something Just Like This

Words and Music by Andrew Taggart,
Chris Martin, Guy Berryman,
Jonny Buckland and Will Champion

78

Stay

Words and Music by Mikky Ekko
and Justin Parker

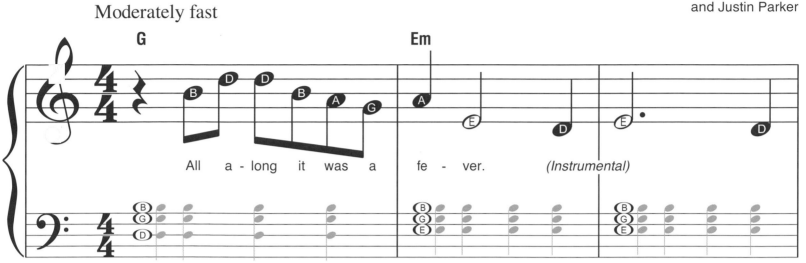

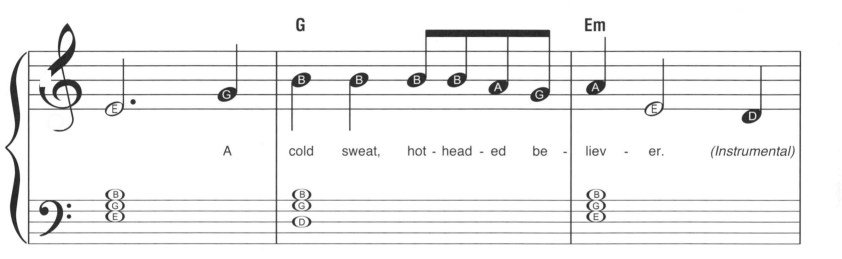

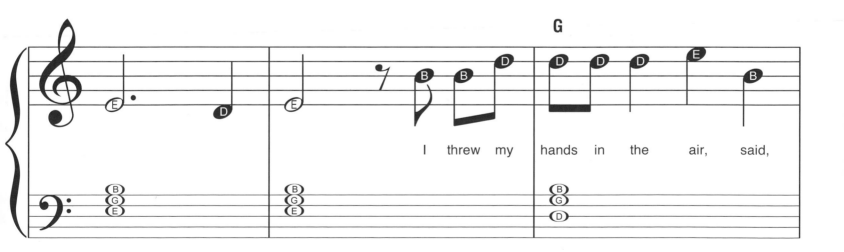

80

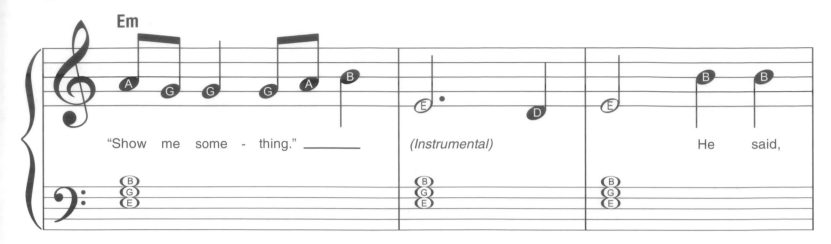

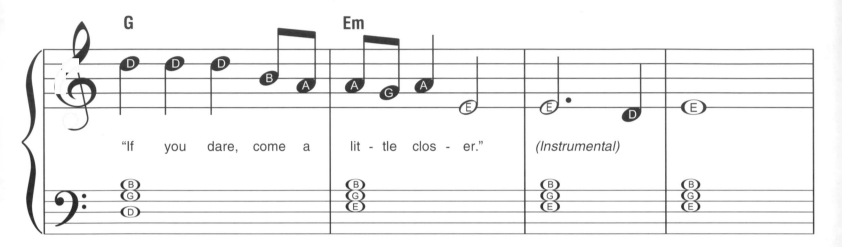

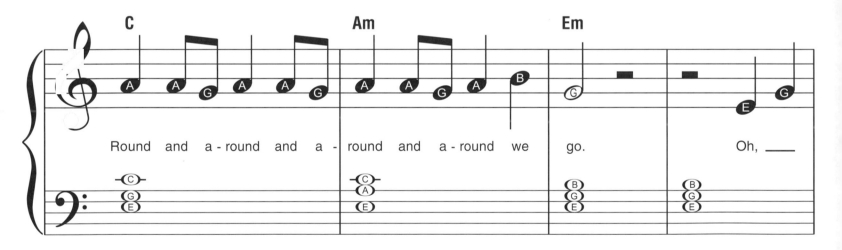

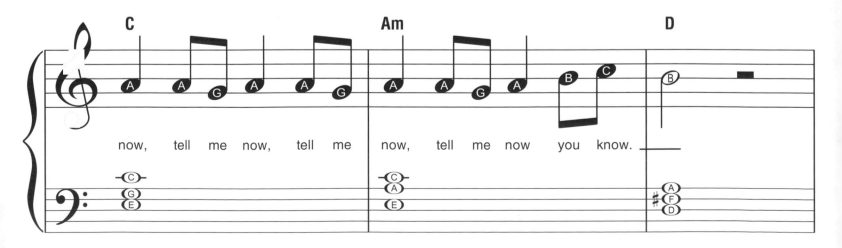

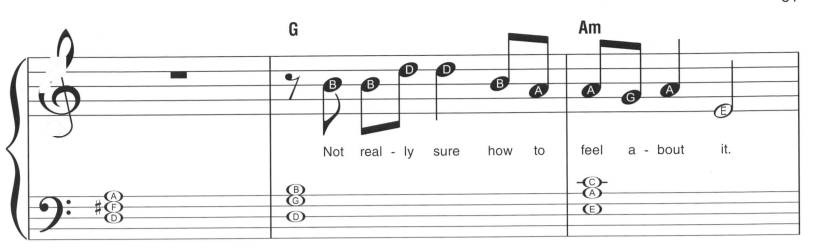

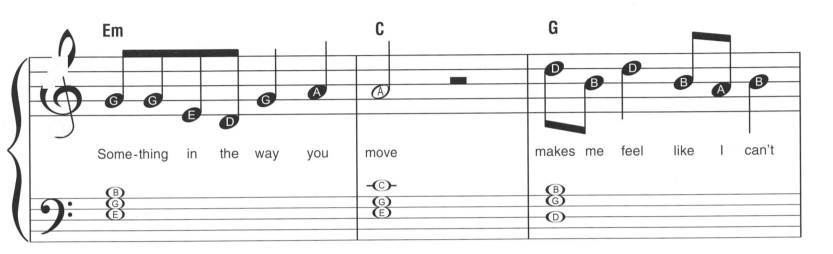

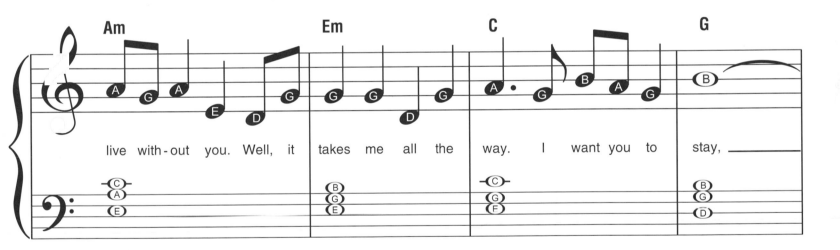

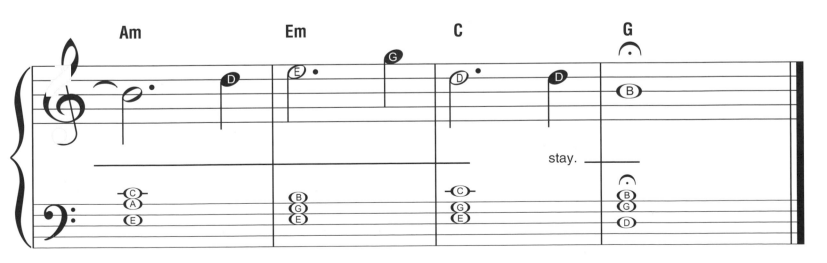

Stitches

Words and Music by Teddy Geiger,
Danny Parker and Daniel Kyriakides

Moderately fast

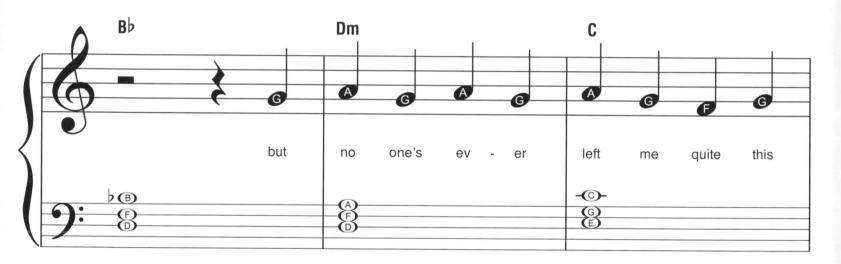

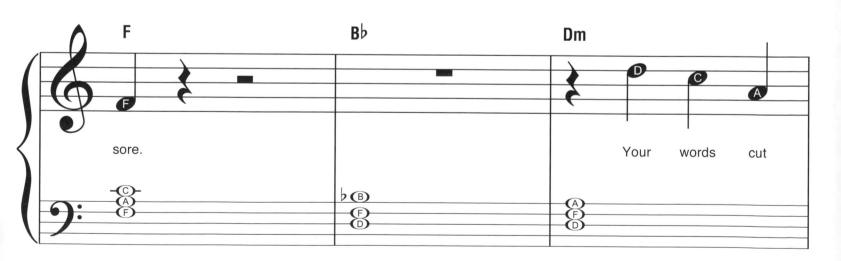

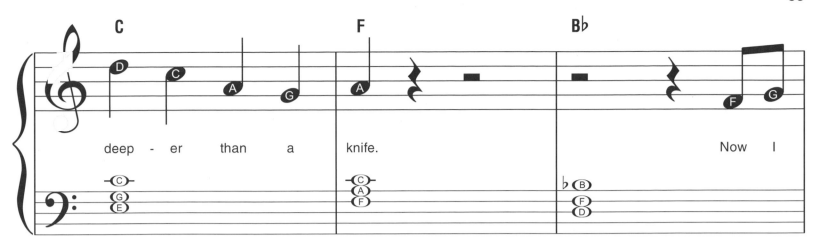

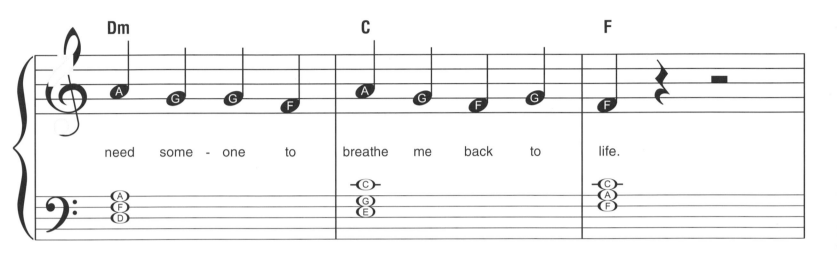

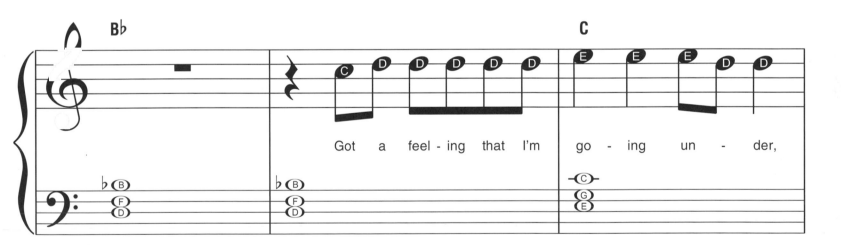

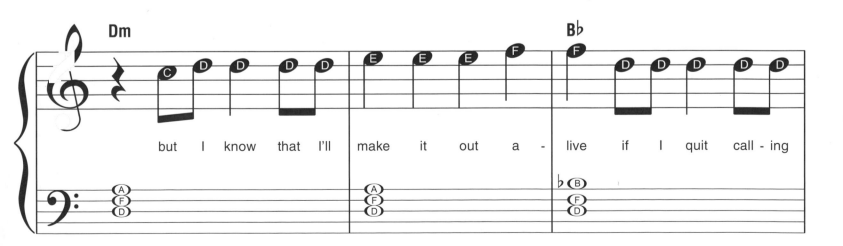

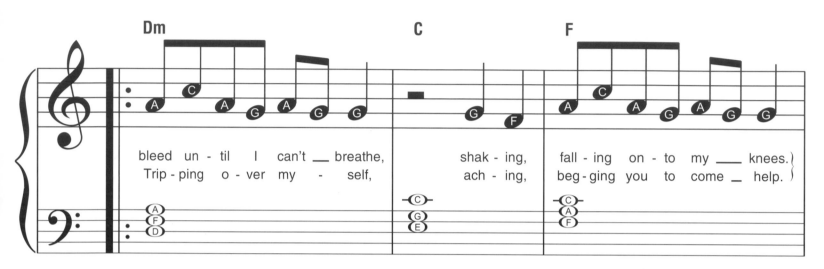

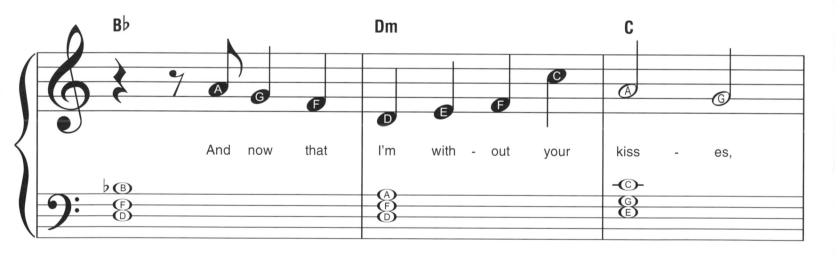

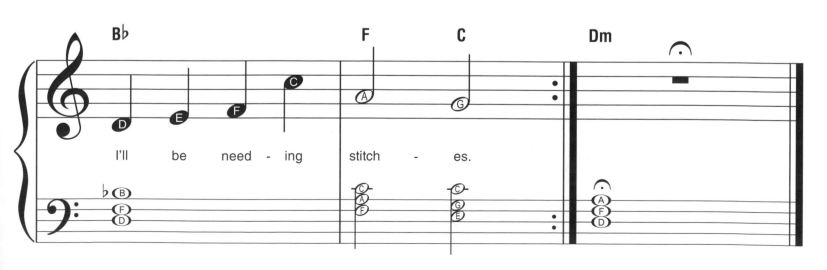

Sucker

Words and Music by Nick Jonas,
Joseph Jonas, Miles Ale,
Ryan Tedder, Louis Bell,
Adam Feeney, Kevin Jonas,
Homer Steinweiss and Mustafa Ahmed

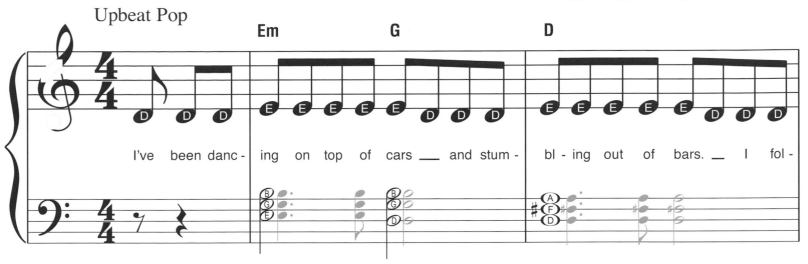

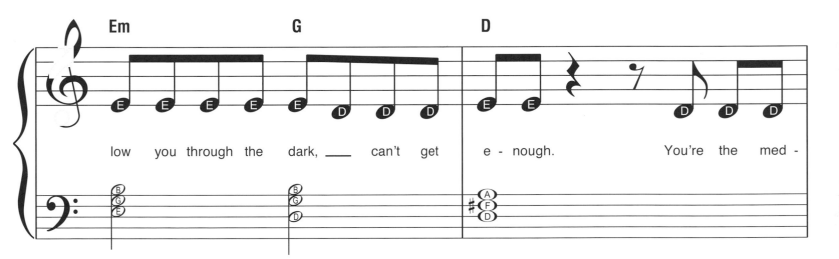

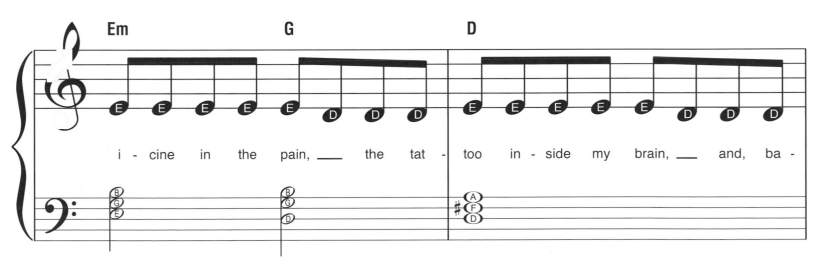

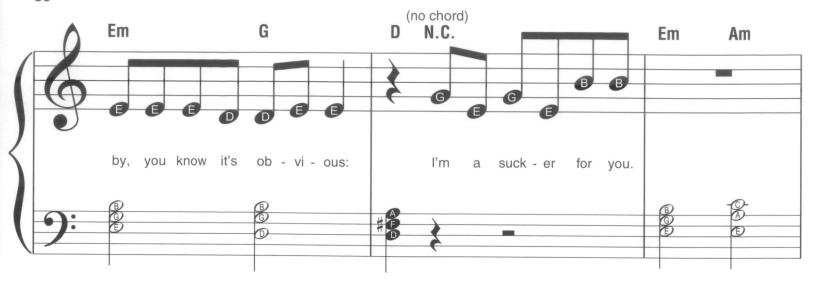

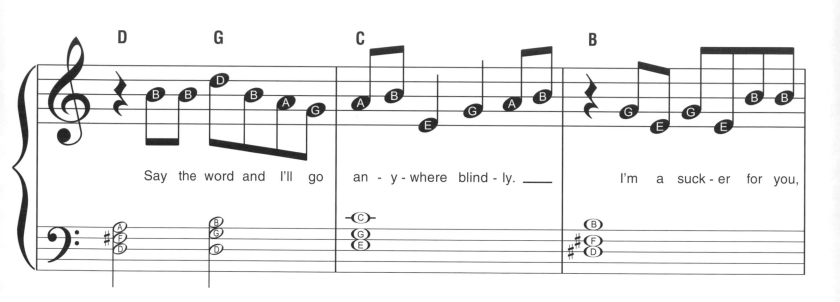

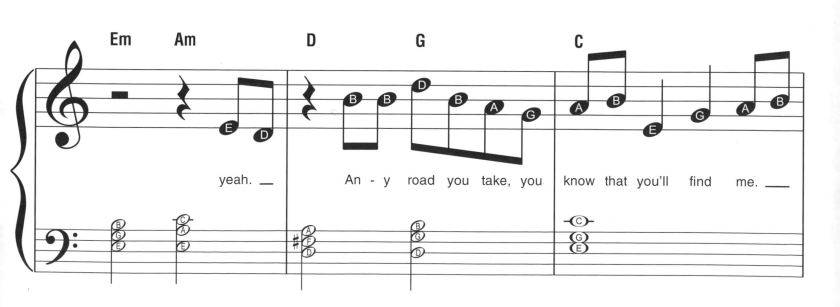

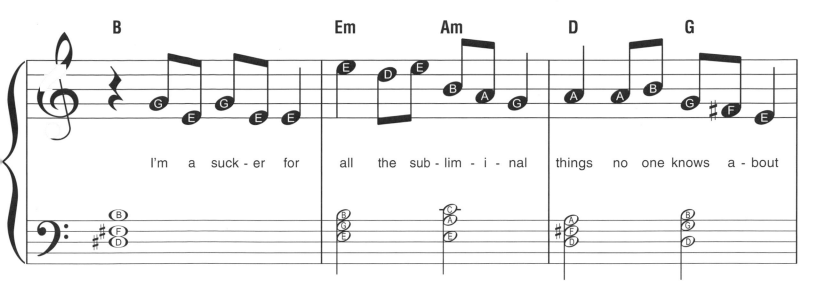

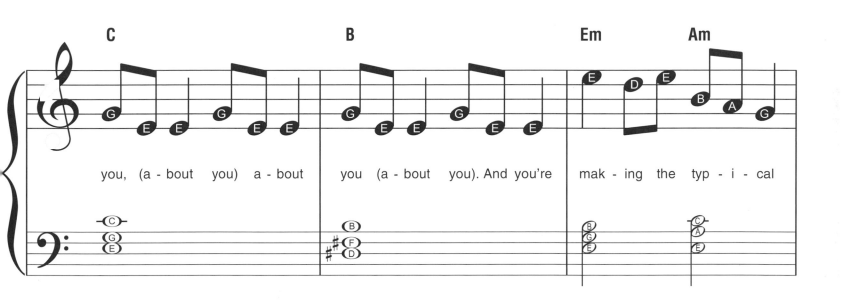

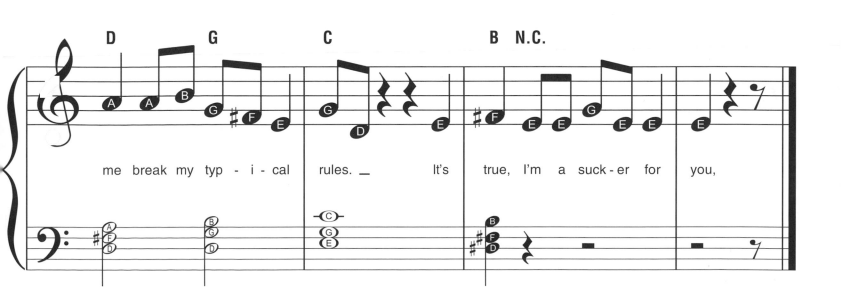

Take Me to Church

Words and Music by
Andrew Hozier-Byrne

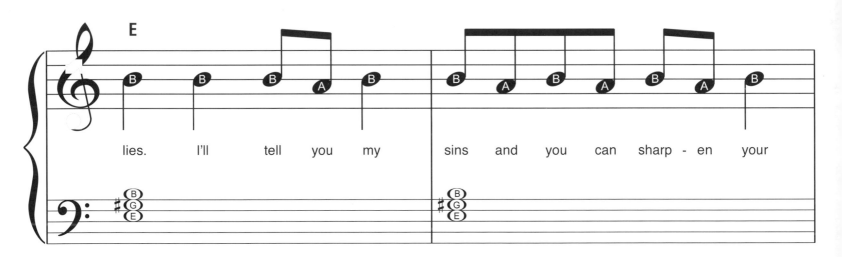

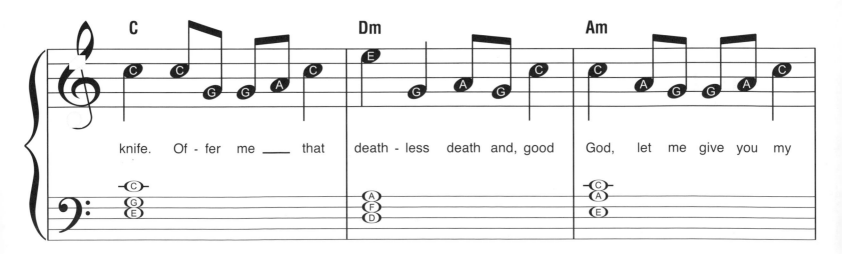

89

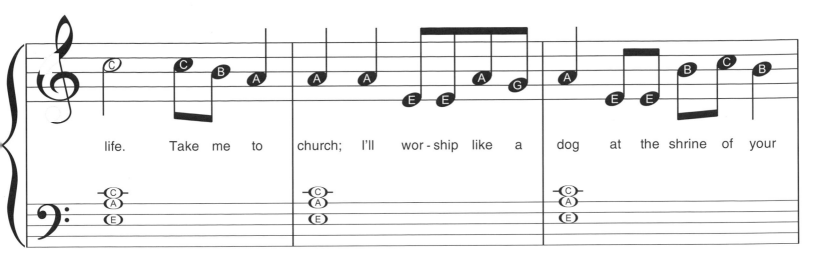

A Thousand Years
from the Summit Entertainment film
THE TWILIGHT SAGA: BREAKING DAWN - PART 1

Words and Music by David Hodges
and Christina Perri

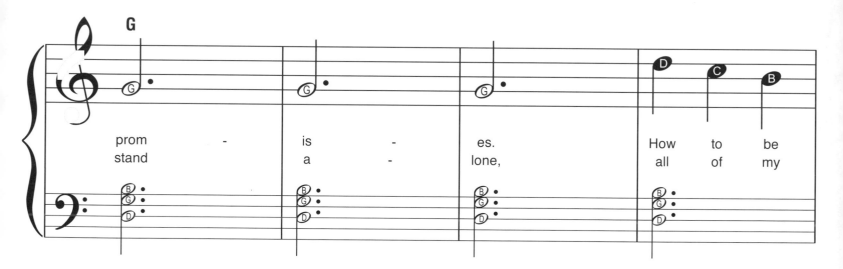

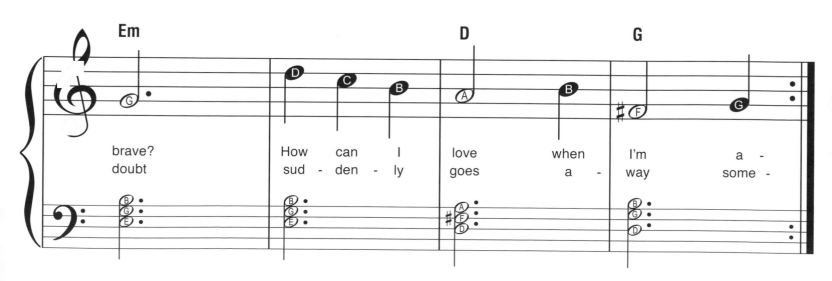

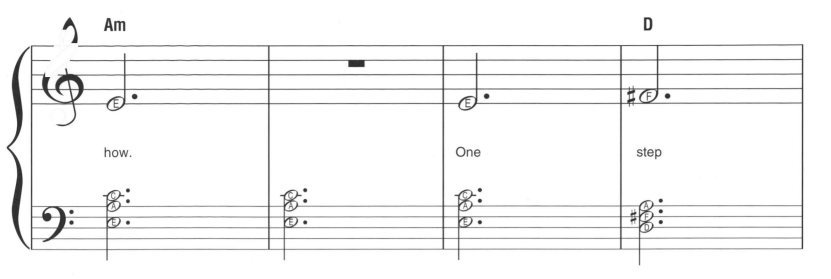

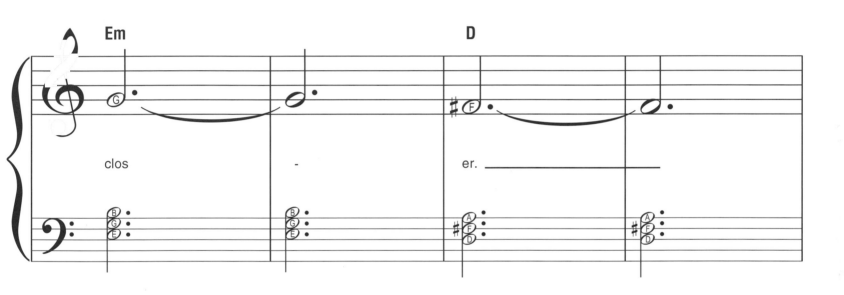

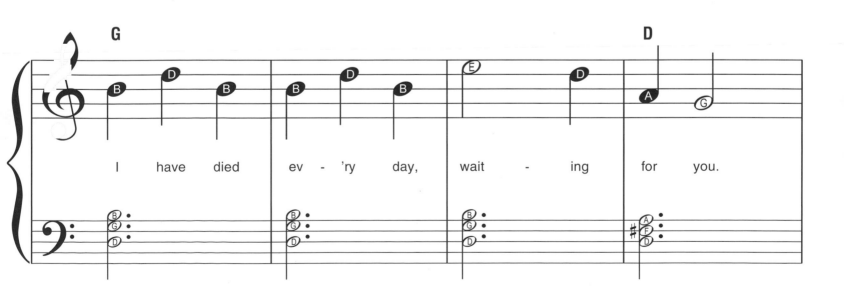

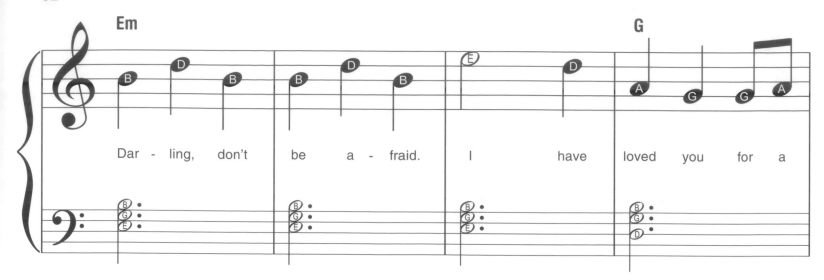

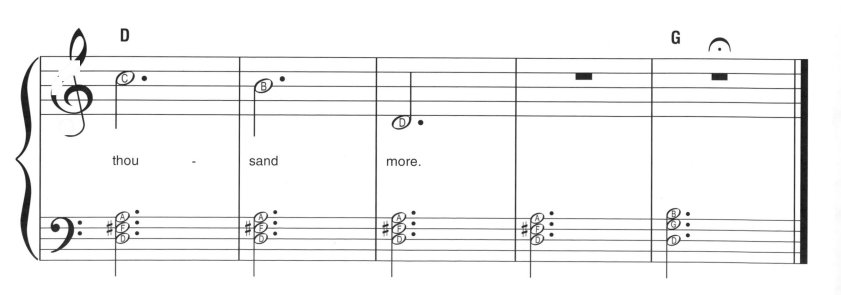

Without Me

Words and Music by Ashley Frangipane,
Brittany Amaradio, Carl Rosen,
Justin Timberlake, Scott Storch,
Louis Bell, Amy Allen
and Timothy Mosley

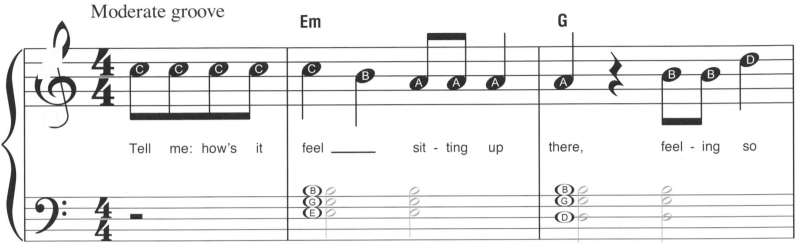

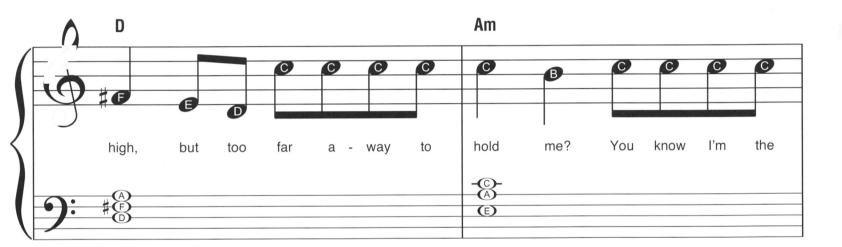

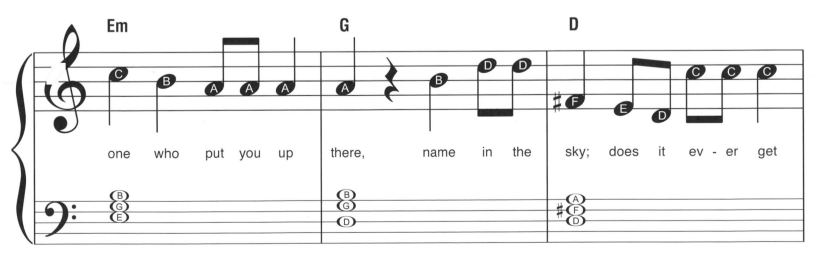

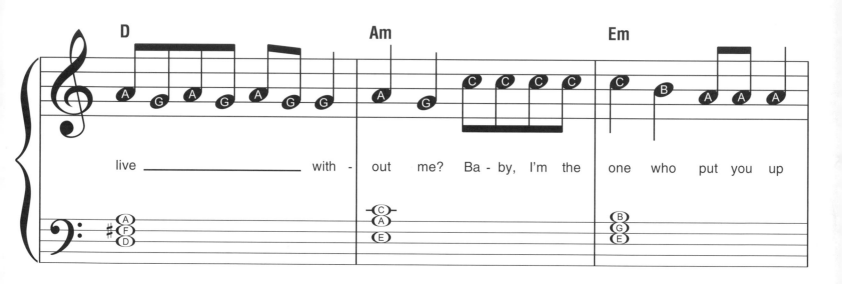

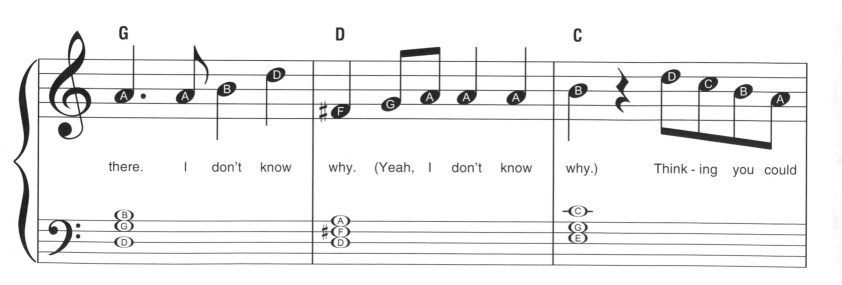

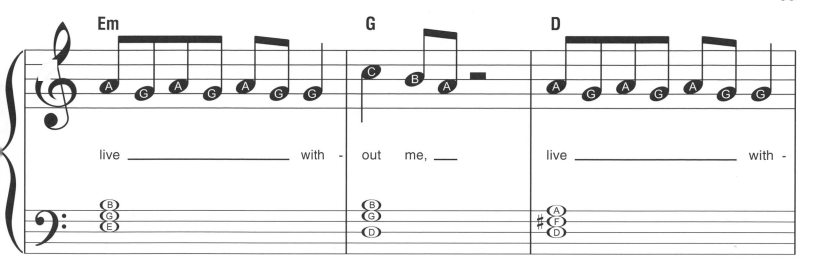

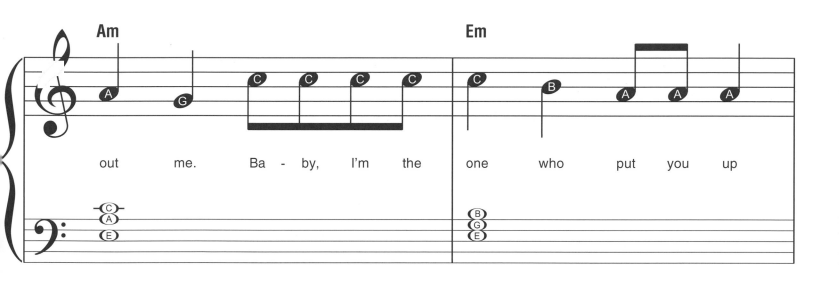

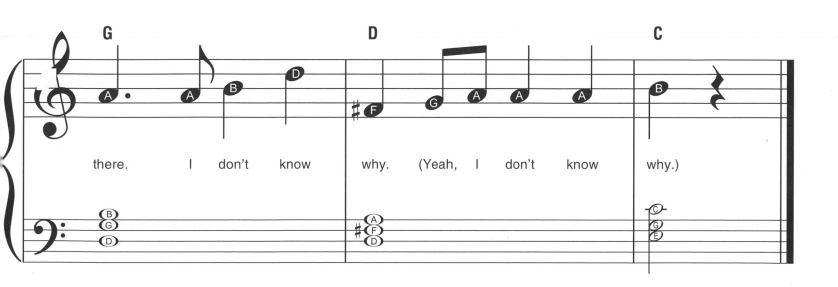

INSTANT Piano Songs

Audio Access
Included

The *Instant Piano Songs* series will help you play your favorite songs quickly and easily — whether you use one hand or two! Start with the melody in your right hand, adding basic left-hand chords when you're ready. Letter names inside each note speed up the learning process, and optional rhythm patterns take your playing to the next level. Online backing tracks are also included. Stream or download the tracks using the unique code inside each book, then play along to build confidence and sound great!

THE BEATLES

All My Loving · Blackbird · Can't Buy Me Love · Eleanor Rigby · Get Back · Here, There and Everywhere · Hey Jude · I Will · Let It Be · Michelle · Nowhere Man · Ob-La-Di, Ob-La-Da · Penny Lane · When I'm Sixty-Four · With a Little Help from My Friends · Yesterday · and more.
00295926 Book/Online Audio $14.99

BROADWAY'S BEST

All I Ask of You · Bring Him Home · Defying Gravity · Don't Cry for Me Argentina · Edelweiss · Memory · The Music of the Night · On My Own · People · Seasons of Love · Send in the Clowns · She Used to Be Mine · Sunrise, Sunset · Tonight · Waving Through a Window · and more.
00323342 Book/Online Audio $14.99

CHRISTMAS CLASSICS

Angels We Have Heard on High · Away in a Manger · Deck the Hall · The First Noel · Good King Wenceslas · Hark! the Herald Angels Sing · Jingle Bells · Jolly Old St. Nicholas · Joy to the World · O Christmas Tree · Up on the Housetop · We Three Kings of Orient Are · We Wish You a Merry Christmas · What Child Is This? · and more.
00348326 Book/Online Audio $14.99

CHRISTMAS STANDARDS

All I Want for Christmas Is You · Christmas Time Is Here · Frosty the Snow Man · Grown-Up Christmas List · A Holly Jolly Christmas · I'll Be Home for Christmas · Jingle Bell Rock · The Little Drummer Boy · Mary, Did You Know? · Merry Christmas, Darling · Rudolph the Red-Nosed Reindeer · White Christmas · and more.
00294854 Book/Online Audio $14.99

CLASSICAL THEMES

Canon (Pachelbel) · Für Elise (Beethoven) · Jesu, Joy of Man's Desiring (Bach) · Jupiter (Holst) · Lullaby (Brahms) · Pomp and Circumstance (Elgar) · Spring (Vivaldi) · Symphony No. 9, Fourth Movement ("Ode to Joy") (Beethoven) · and more.
00283826 Book/Online Audio $14.99

DISNEY FAVORITES

Beauty and the Beast · Can You Feel the Love Tonight · Chim Chim Cher-ee · Colors of the Wind · A Dream Is a Wish Your Heart Makes · Friend Like Me · How Far I'll Go · It's a Small World · Kiss the Girl · Lava · Let It Go · Mickey Mouse March · Part of Your World · Reflection · Remember Me (Ernesto de la Cruz) · A Whole New World · You'll Be in My Heart (Pop Version) · and more.
00283720 Book/Online Audio $14.99

HITS OF 2010-2019

All About That Bass (Meghan Trainor) · All of Me (John Legend) · Can't Stop the Feeling (Justin Timberlake) · Happy (Pharrell Williams) · Hey, Soul Sister (Train) · Just the Way You Are (Bruno Mars) · Rolling in the Deep (Adele) · Shallow (Lady Gaga & Bradley Cooper) · Shake It Off (Taylor Swift) · Shape of You (Ed Sheeran) · and more.
00345364 Book/Online Audio $14.99

KIDS' POP SONGS

Adore You (Harry Styles) · Cool Kids (AJR) · Drivers License (Olivia Rodrigo) · How Far I'll Go (from Moana) · A Million Dreams (from The Greatest Showman) · Ocean Eyes (Billie Eilish) · Shake It Off (Taylor Swift) · What Makes You Beautiful (One Direction) · and more.
00371694 Book/Online Audio $14.99

MOVIE SONGS

As Time Goes By · City of Stars · Endless Love · Hallelujah · I Will Always Love You · Laura · Moon River · My Heart Will Go on (Love Theme from 'Titanic') · Over the Rainbow · Singin' in the Rain · Skyfall · Somewhere Out There · Stayin' Alive · Tears in Heaven · Unchained Melody · Up Where We Belong · The Way We Were · What a Wonderful World · and more.
00283718 Book/Online Audio $14.99

POP HITS

All of Me · Chasing Cars · Despacito · Feel It Still · Havana · Hey, Soul Sister · Ho Hey · I'm Yours · Just Give Me a Reason · Love Yourself · Million Reasons · Perfect · Riptide · Shake It Off · Stay with Me · Thinking Out Loud · Viva La Vida · What Makes You Beautiful · and more.
00283825 Book/Online Audio $15.99

SONGS FOR KIDS

Do-Re-Mi · Hakuna Matata · It's a Small World · On Top of Spaghetti · Puff the Magic Dragon · The Rainbow Connection · SpongeBob SquarePants Theme Song · Take Me Out to the Ball Game · Tomorrow · The Wheels on the Bus · Won't You Be My Neighbor? (It's a Beautiful Day in the Neighborhood) · You Are My Sunshine · and more.
00323352 Book/Online Audio $15.99

www.halleonard.com